Every Road
Goes
Somewhere

"In this thoughtful, vulnerable memoir, Wendy invites us to see our own socially acceptable addictions for gaining security and significance, which we frequently baptize in our pursuit of faithfulness: our fretful striving to discern God's will, our passion to be useful and necessary in the kingdom, and our drive to be high-achieving stewards of God's gifts. Her journey bids us to discover a longed-for rest in God's faithfulness, love, and grace—to know the God who turns dead ends into new beginnings and who keeps intimate company with us along every twist and turn of the journey."

Sharon Garlough Brown, author of the Sensible Shoes series and the Shades of Light series

"Proverbs likens life to a path. Wisdom is necessary to navigate the unexpected twists and turns that life often brings. Wendy Widder beautifully tells us the story of her journey in *Every Road Goes Somewhere*. She does us the honor of making herself vulnerable and inviting us into her story. Through her observant reflections, she shares with us her persistent faith in the face of disappointment and joy so we too can gain encouragement and insight as we walk on our life path. Thank you, Wendy, for this powerful memoir."

Tremper Longman III, PhD, Distinguished Scholar and Professor Emeritus of Biblical Studies, Westmont College

"Wendy's memoir is an important reminder that even scholars who spend their lives studying and teaching the Bible are not immune from life's struggles, disappointments, and challenges. Her story reminds us that every believer—including biblical and theological scholars—has flaws and blind spots in their theology and more to learn, that God calls all children to be lifelong learners. He redeems life's ups and downs to take us to deeper levels of understanding and trust in the God who loves us."

Carolyn Custis James, author of *Half the Church: Recapturing God's Global Vision for Women* and *Malestrom: How Jesus Dismantles Patriarchy and Redefines Manhood*; www.carolyncustisjames.com

"I read *Every Road Goes Somewhere* in one sitting. For someone who normally has a dozen or more books in process, that is remarkable. Wendy Widder's very personal and vulnerable story holds your attention as you travel with her on her very relatable journey. Her love for and skill with words is evident and captivating. Despite stellar scholarly credentials, her conversational style is engagingly accessible. Anyone who grew up in an evangelical culture will especially identify with a great deal of her story. Readers will be greatly helped by Wendy's transparency about friendship, singleness, disappointment, anxiety, and shattered expectations. She weaves the maturing of her faith and of her understanding of God and his ways into her story in ways that are not preachy but intensely helpful."

Dr. Bill Rudd, pastor, professor, and author

"What happens when your sincerest childhood aptitudes and aspirations are exactly suited to each other, suited to the context that raised you, and then you discover God didn't get the memo? Wendy Widder invites us to join her on her own journey from precocious childhood through the baffling twists, turns, disappointments, and even devastations of following a God who loved her too much to relinquish her to assumptions, tradition, or the religious American dream. Instead, this God—through life events and human companions, but largely through the pages of the Bible—challenged her to live a life of genuine faith. A life where her God-given skills have been honed and used but she could not fall back on them alone, but had to trust the God who gave them to her for every step. From all accounts, she is still doing it. Her book shows us that even if and when the end result remains unseen, following God is worth it."

Jennifer A. G. Layte, author, spiritual director, pastor

A
MEMOIR
ABOUT
CALLING

Every Road Goes Somewhere

WENDY WIDDER

Three Rubies Press
Farmington, Minnesota

© 2022 by Wendy Widder
Published by Three Rubies Press
Farmington, MN 55024
https://wendywidder.com

ISBN 979-8-9864408-0-4 (paperback)
ISBN 979-8-9864408-1-1 (e-book)

Library of Congress Control Number: 2022913492

This book is a memoir. It reflects the author's present recollections of experiences over time. Most names have been changed, and some characteristics have been altered. Some events have been compressed, and some dialogue has been recreated.

Editor: Gisèle Mix

Cover design: Black Kat Design

Interior design: Bree Rose Creative
Interior art: Black Kat Design

Printed in the United States of America

First paperback edition November 2022

Unless otherwise indicated, Scripture quotations are from the King James Version of the Bible.

To my family and friend after friend
who walked these roads with me,
and to Rick, who helped me cross the ford.

My story is important not because it is mine, God knows, but because if I tell it anything like right, the chances are you will recognize that in many ways it is also yours. . . . It is precisely through these stories in all their particularity . . . that God makes himself known to each of us more powerfully and personally. If this is true, it means that to lose track of our stories is to be profoundly impoverished not only humanly but also spiritually.

Frederick Buechner, *Telling Secrets*

CONTENTS

INTRODUCTION

My high school geography class spent a lot of time making maps. Topographic maps, road maps, political maps. The capstone project was to invent an island and create a map for it, synthesizing various elements of mapmaking—scale, contour lines and corresponding topography, settlements, natural resources, and so on.

I made plenty of mistakes on my island map—drawing rivers where they couldn't possibly flow, positioning villages in unsustainable environments, and misjudging the likelihood of natural resources. My map even included extra "local color"—a grease stain from the butter dish on the kitchen table.

Turns out, inventing geography, even in two dimensions, is harder than it sounds. It's a lot easier to draw maps of places that already exist, places I've been to or studied in books.

This book is a map of my life and one I couldn't see very clearly until I'd followed its meandering path to and, more importantly, *out of* a midlife abyss. Along the way, I thought I knew where the map would take me, but I had it all wrong. Well-meaning people often told me where it was going. But they were wrong too.

We all have different maps—designed by Someone with a much better lay of the land than we have. Some maps have pristine beaches

1

and crystal water. Some have steep hills and deep valleys, plunging cliffs and churning waves. Most include dense forests, expansive wilderness, and soaring peaks. The Mapmaker puts paths where we never would and erects mountains where we'd have put a highway.

This divine mapmaking is wrapped up with questions of calling and vocation, topics of perennial interest in the church: What is God calling me to do with my life? How can I find the right, nay, the *perfect* fit for my passions and abilities? Where, in the words of Frederick Buechner, do my "deep gladness and the world's deep hunger meet"?[1]

What sometimes gets lost in these questions is that most maps go places we didn't expect—and not always good places, at least as we'd define good. Some journeys are marked more by disappointment than accomplishment. We forget that the world is broken—that our individual worlds are broken—and following Jesus doesn't change that.

Our maps may all look different, but despite these variations, all the roads we travel matter because God made the map, butter stains and all.

THE MAP

*N*orth-south-east-west would come—and go—later. The points on my compass as a child were more concrete, destinations I could reach on my own two legs: Killer Hill, the Boy Blue ice cream shop, Maude Shunk Library, and Thomas Jefferson Elementary School. At the center of my compass was our house on Shady Lane, a three-bedroom ranch that my parents built in one of the baby boom subdivisions of suburban Milwaukee.

Situated on a short end of a long block, our house sat between the Murphys and the Browns. The Murphys had a dog and the Browns had a baby, but neither had children my age; for that I had to either cross the street to Jillian Lee's house or head out the back gate to my best friend's house. Jillian's main draw was a Big Wheel, but Holly had a Hasbro bouncy Inchworm, a spring rocking horse, a sandbox, and junk food. Holly's house smelled like cat litter and cigarette smoke, but I considered that a small price to pay for Hostess Twinkies and Doritos.

Most of the time, I played at home with my older sister Suzy, my parents' surprise baby. She was born five years after my brother and eight years after my oldest sister, Bonnie. When I came squalling into the world one Sunday afternoon three years after Suzy, my dad was at church teaching an adult Bible class. Summoned to the hallway pay phone, he took the call from my mom, returned to class, and without speaking a word wrote on the chalkboard, "It's a girl."

Months before I arrived, my mom's doctor had told her to expect a Christmas baby. She told him in no uncertain terms that I would be born before December 1. What she actually said was "This baby is going to school when she's four." The school district's cutoff birth date for four-year-olds to start kindergarten was December 1; any babies born after that had to wait until the following September when they were five. I suppose by child number four, my mom was ready to have the house to herself for a few hours every weekday, and sure enough, I was born Thanksgiving weekend.

Suzy and I were best of friends, most days anyway, playing Barbies and Matchbox cars, racing down the hallway on all fours, and sledding down the basement stairs on an old couch cushion. In the basement we roller-skated loops through my dad's workroom and the laundry room, and we played house in the three-room playhouse Dad had built to match the house that sat over it: white siding, maroon trim, and real shingles. Outside we swung like monkeys on the backyard swing set, made forts with blankets slung over the clothesline, and joined neighborhood kids for fifty-scatter, a '70s version of hide-and-seek.

Shady Lane was a quiet street that made a wide curve onto Alfred Place, leaving behind a sort of cul-de-sac that was the perfect space for neighborhood games of kickball. Our house was a block removed from a primary neighborhood attraction: Killer Hill, an intense slope for winter sledding and summer rolling. Around our block the other direction was a main thoroughfare through the subdivision, a road we ran across after looking both ways twice. One summer after a car hit a girl crossing the street on her bike, we started looking three times before crossing.

My dad liked to walk the neighborhood for exercise and probably his own sanity, and we often accompanied him. I suspect his taking one or two, and sometimes three or four, children for a walk served a dual purpose for our single-income family: he could spend time with us and also reprieve my stay-at-home mom from, well, spending time with us. One of our favorite destinations was the Boy Blue ice cream shop in the commercial plaza along the four-lane main street into town. The seven blocks of sidewalk between our house and Boy Blue were enough to make the walk itself most of the outing. Along the way we'd compete to see who could kick the same rock for the longest stretch of sidewalk, or one of us would skip ahead and then wait for everyone to catch up, and for sure we'd chatter about the important decision that lay ahead: which flavor of ice cream.

Along the route one afternoon, I noticed slashes of paint on the sidewalks, and I asked my dad what they were for. Rather than simply answering my question, he suggested we form a hypothesis.

"A what?" I asked. I was probably school age at the time, but the curriculum at Thomas Jefferson hadn't reached the scientific method yet.

Dad went on, telling me to observe where the slashes occurred and notice what similarities the locations had. For the next couple of blocks, I paid closer attention to the slashes and the sidewalks and soon concluded that all the sidewalks with paint had cracks.

"Why do you think there's a paint mark on those sidewalks? What do you think the paint means? That's your hypothesis." He went on to explain how to test a hypothesis and either discard it or move toward a theory if there was enough evidence.

I walked and talked many miles of sidewalk with my dad in the years that followed this trip to Boy Blue, but this lesson in the scientific method is the only conversation I clearly remember. When he could have simply told me that city crews were preparing to replace broken sidewalks in the neighborhood, he instead taught me how to see the world. Observe things in context. Reflect on them. Test your ideas. Be willing to be wrong. Try again.

My dad was a lifelong educator. By the time I caboosed my way into the family, he was moving into his second career with the Milwaukee Public Schools. After teaching fifth grade for eleven years, he became a school psychologist. I never had the chance to ask him what prompted this career change, but if my own decision to do something similar years later at all reflected his, it may have been that he got bored. That he earned both a master's degree and a doctorate in the course of his career suggests he needed a different kind of challenge than shepherding an annual herd of ten-year-olds through fractions and long division, state capitals and the solar system.

But he never stopped teaching, and my siblings and I were his perpetual students. A 1972 set of World Book encyclopedias was our Google, and a 1960s set of Childcraft encyclopedias was our go-to source of nursery rhymes, poems, and classic stories. The illustration of a rabid Old Yeller lunging against the shed door was usually more than I could take, and most of my Childcraft hours were spent with volumes 1 and 2, collections of softly illustrated nursery rhymes and other poems.

We loved words. My sister Bonnie read the dictionary for fun, but we all loved a delicious word like *discombobulation*. Some words were just more fun to say if you shifted the accent or adjusted the pronunciation, so *obstacle* in our house was usually *ob-STA-cle*, *Menards* was *MAY-nerds*, and *vehicle* was *VE-HI-cle*. When the eye doctor prescribed distance-reading practice for Suzy, my dad and brother created eye charts for her. They set their handiwork on the shelf of the secretary, and while Suzy read each card from across the dinette, the two of them waited with wry grins: U R A Q T; U N I R N A C; and C D M T C.

This love of wordplay explains one of my favorite books at Maude Shunk Library (known in our family as "Mad Skunk," with no disrespect whatsoever meant to the matriarch of the community library, a bespectacled white-haired lady whose picture stood guard over the main lobby). On the cover of the book, a white-bearded king dressed like Father Christmas hovered horizontally in midair while rain poured from him: *The King Who Rained*, written and illustrated by Fred Gwynne, a.k.a. Herman Munster, the lovable star of the 1960s sitcom *The Munsters*. The book follows a little girl through the bewildering and hilarious world of homonyms and idioms in her parents' speech: there were forks in the road; Daddy (who bore a remarkable likeness to Herman Munster) had a mole on his nose; Mommy's throat was a little horse; Daddy had a frog in his throat. The book was better checked out and read at home where giggles and howls didn't bring a stern look from the librarian.

The library was an easy walk due west of our house, and it was a destination Suzy and I were allowed to go unaccompanied. During the summer months, we'd eat our Corn Flakes and drink our Tang and then set out with our tattered library cards and bag of books. Turning left at the end of the driveway, we walked two blocks to where our street dead-ended at the outfield of a community ball field. Squeezing through the fence, we'd trot to home plate and then continue past the bleachers along the lot line with the Lutheran church to the frontage road that led to the library's back entrance. The library had two entrances—the main entrance that opened into the adult library upstairs and our entrance, the downstairs back one that landed us in the children's library, where we returned one bag of books and spent the morning in search of its replacement.

As the sun passed overhead, Suzy and I would venture upstairs and head straight for the farthest corner of the reading room where a box of comic books invited us into the adventures of Archie and Jughead, Veronica and Betty, and the rest of Riverdale. We must have gone home for lunch and maybe even stayed there—but in my memories, hours spent in the library and hours spent at home merge into one. The library was home, so much so that one morning when Suzy and I arrived before the doors were unlocked, as we often did, and saw a new sign on the downstairs door, we knew we were both its cause and target: No Bare Feet.

When adolescence drew Suzy into the privacy of her own bedroom, I often went to the library by myself. *The King Who Rained* gave way to Nancy Drew, but the library and its books were still my wardrobe to Narnia, the place from which I ventured into new worlds. In the pages of hundreds of books, I scampered about places like Plum Creek and Avonlea, surrounded by friends like Ramona, Encyclopedia Brown, and Bilbo. Books opened up new worlds to be explored, with everything to gain and nothing to lose.

But my love for books was about more than just vicarious experiences and adventure. It was about a love of knowledge, an unquenchable thirst for information and learning and putting the world together. Books were where I went to learn about things I just wanted to know or about things I was too shy or embarrassed to ask. When my parents decided it was time for me to know about the birds and the bees, I was given a little paperback book and instructions from my mom to ask her any questions I might have. I didn't have any. At least that's what I thought until, sometime after the little book was buried in the deepest, darkest corner of a dresser drawer, I found myself confused by junior high "locker room talk." I actually had lots of questions, but there was no way I was going to ask my mom. Instead, I went to the 1972 World Book, where I realized—with not a little preteen horror—that either the book my parents gave me had skipped some important information or I had somehow missed it (which inexplicably was, I later learned, the case). Although the 1972 World Book was outdated in many ways by the time I sought out this information, it was still spot on with its article about the birds and bees.

I often turned to books for information about my body—or bodies in general. Our family acquired a two-volume medical dictionary about the time I was learning about sex from World Book, and I asked it lots of questions. My mom usually said my pains were growing pains, but I wasn't so sure. When I had frequent headaches, I went in search of a cause other than the brain tumor I most feared (my dad's twin died from a brain tumor when they were nine). When my legs hurt, I asked the medical dictionary if my leg would need to be amputated like the neighbor girl's. If my jaw hurt, I asked if TMJ is hereditary. Even though the diagnoses I gave myself were often terminal, I couldn't tear myself away from the lure of knowledge, following one trail after another through the medical dictionary.

I loved books because they let me ask questions and process answers at my own speed. They let me follow a meandering path to wherever I ended up—and I rarely knew where that would be. The reward was the journey.

School capitalized on this hunger for books and learning, but it offered me more than the reward of the journey; it also gave me the reward of destinations, clear marks of achievement.

The lure of achievement grabbed me, so I loved school from the first day Suzy and I turned right instead of left at the end of the driveway on weekday mornings. We'd zigzag seven blocks through the neighborhood to the edge of the Thomas Jefferson playground, which butted up against the ball fields of the high school where we took summer swimming lessons. My kindergarten classroom looked out on the playground, and Miss Moore was my teacher until she added a syllable to her name at midyear, becoming Mrs. Morehead. After kindergarten, I crossed the hall to the Misses Carter, two sisters who taught first and second grade. Miss Carter the First was the shorter of the pair, her jet-black hair perfectly coifed to frame a wide-set face and full cheeks. She wore knee-length dresses, and her shoes clicked on the tile floor. Miss Carter the Second had short brown hair with an unruly wave, the right combination with the pants and button-down shirts she typically wore.

In three years of progress reports from Thomas Jefferson, there are only two categories with check marks in the "Needs Attention" column: writing legibly and knowing the "required addition and subtraction facts." The deficit in math appears early in second grade and quickly changes to "Excellent Progress," though I never did master the penmanship problem (though at least Miss Carter said it "Shows Progress"). I tolerated handwriting and worked hard at math, but reading was by far my strongest subject, as Miss Carter the First noted to my parents on her final report: "I don't have to tell you to encourage her to read."

The avid reader that Miss Carter the First promoted to her sister's class down the hall was well prepared to shine when a class reading contest was announced. On one of the classroom's large bulletin boards, Miss Carter the Second stapled an oversized cutout of a floppy-eared dog. Positioned along the bottom edge of the board was a row of construction paper dog bones, each with a student's name in teacher-perfect penmanship. Every time we reported having read a book, she would write its title on a smaller dog bone and staple it above our names. The student with the biggest pile of dog bones won.

Miss Carter the First's end-of-the-year praise aside, this was an easy contest to win for a little girl who lived in the local library while summer waxed and waned. But it was even easier because I cheated—that is, until my dad realized the error of my ways. After I had devoured every book we had at home within two years of my reading level, my dad and I hunted and gathered books from the library by the bagful. We took them home, and I read them. Or, I should say, I "read" them. I didn't so much *devour* these books as *lick* them or *sniff* them. With a pile of books on my left, I'd pick one off the top of the pile, open its front cover, and turn every page until the end—scanning my eyes across the pictures and words with a single left-to-right swipe. I'd deposit the book on another pile and reach for the next book. Somewhere along the way, my dad discovered his little second grader's reading method and gently set me straight: if the book was going to count for the contest, I actually had to *read* it. So I did. Every one of them.

I don't think there was any question at home or in my second-grade class that I would win the contest (fair and square). It wasn't even a contest: my dog bone pile soared and toppled in the leftover spaces above my classmates' names.

From Miss Moore/Mrs. Morehead's half-day kindergarten until I gave the valedictory address at high school graduation, I loved nearly everything about school. Sure, there were always classmates who tried my patience—like Billy Boondocker, who ran around our unsupervised second-grade classroom one afternoon wagging his first-grade stuff through his unzipped fly. And there were teachers whose methods were maddening or whose expectations were unclear, such as Miss Larsen, who gave me a C in tenth-grade PE because I wasn't an extrovert (what she really said was that she thought I could show more enthusiasm for the various activities we did), or Mr. Duncan, who wandered around topics as if he were lost in the fog. But bothersome classmates and frustrating teachers came and went. My only perennial disappointment in school was the hand-me-down box of crayons in my school supplies.

While my love for the library and my love for school were closely related and even complementary, they had one key difference: the library had no expectations of me, except that I wear my shoes; school, however, was full of expectations, usually clearly defined. And these expectations formed a ladder of achievement to climb.

This didn't bother me since I never met a school rung I could not climb (except for high school chemistry, which left me so baffled after two weeks that I dropped it, a decision I still regret). I often saw a rung as a challenge to go beyond, to climb another rung. School gave direction to my curiosity and creativity, and I thrived—in the journey and the destination, the learning itself and the achievements.

School—and my insatiable appetite for it—shaped me in ways I didn't realize until I was much older. Like the other neighborhood destinations that oriented my childhood, school defined my sense of who I am and what my place is in the world.

Another destination wasn't reachable on foot, but its circumscription of my life was just as clear: church, and specifically, our conservative Baptist church.

The steepled building that housed our church was almost a second home while I was growing up. The church's weekly schedule anchored our weeks, beginning with Sunday morning when the Widder family piled into our silver-gray Chevrolet station wagon—three in the front and three in the back, seatbelts optional. Since I was the youngest and smallest, I always had one of the two middle seats, either between Dad driving and Mom blotting her lipstick in the visor mirror or in the back between my brother and my oldest sister, doing her own teenage primping in her compact mirror.

Twenty minutes later, Dad pulled "the Silver Bullet" up to the front entrance of the sprawling redbrick building. We tumbled out, and once inside I raced through the labyrinth of cinder-block hallways to find my Sunday school room. A secretary smiled her greeting and marked my attendance, and I made my way through the room that was teeming with teachers—mostly women—readying the morning's materials. At my assigned table, I chattered with Sunday-morning friends while we colored and cut, glued and stapled, and recited the week's memory verse. The first bell signaled the official start of Sunday school, thirty minutes that included prayer requests, a flannelgraph lesson, and a worksheet activity.

When the second bell rang, we scooped up our papers—bound for the refrigerator at home—and scurried to the main area for children's church. For the next thirty minutes (or more if the sermon upstairs went long), we sang songs written with black marker on poster board, dropped grimy coins in an offering basket, and listened to a second Bible lesson. Children's church in the Primary room often included mini-lessons on elements of Big Church: What is worship? What is an offering—and why do we give one? What is a missionary? Once or twice a year, we'd even have a real live missionary in children's church. In the older grades of the Junior room, the highlight was a Bible drill competition or Bible quiz.

After church, our family went home for a quiet Sunday afternoon—naps, whether we wanted them or not, maybe some golf on TV (because it was the right pace for Sunday), and a walk to Boy Blue if we were lucky. Then at 6:30, earlier if there was children's choir practice, Dad pulled the Silver Bullet out of the garage again, and we headed back for the Sunday evening service.

Without poster-board songs, flannelgraph lessons, or Bible drills, I relied on people-watching from a pew to pass the sixty-minute service. Mr. Johnson tugging at his unruly eyebrows. Mrs. Bigelow clickety-clacking her nail clipper during the sermon. Mr. Harvey nodding and bobbing until the final "Amen." The best part about the Sunday evening service came after the closing hymn, when Mr. Pafford, the grandfatherly head usher, buoyed the small survivors of Sunday night church with soft toffees from his pocket.

Thus went the first day of the week for the Widders. The three days that followed meant work and school, but after supper on Wednesday, we piled back into the station wagon for the twenty-minute trip to prayer meeting. By midweek, the frenzied buzz of Sunday had dulled to barely a hum. Pastor Sawyer clipped on his lapel mic and moved from the platform pulpit to a lectern on the floor. After leading the faithful in a hymn or two and offering a brief devotional, he opened the floor for prayer requests, followed by what felt like hours of praying. Since only Pastor Sawyer had a microphone, many of the prayers were far-off murmurs interspersed with long periods of silence until the next volunteer stood to pray. Pastor Sawyer's closing prayer mercifully signaled the end of the service, and when he said "Amen," I was off in search (and need) of Mr. Pafford's toffee.

Sunday and Wednesday services were year-round stays in our schedule. During the school year, Awana Club on Friday nights was too. Awana, an acronym for "Approved Workmen Are Not Ashamed" (derived from 2 Tim. 2:15), is a baptized (and largely Baptist) version of Scouts that focuses on Bible memorization. When I was growing up, its clubs began in third grade with Chums for girls and Pals for boys. My dad directed the Pals when my parents were first married. When my mom began a thirteen-year stint as director of Chums a few years later, he stayed home with us until we were old enough to attend ourselves.

We were at church whenever the bulletin said we could be. And we were there even when it didn't. My mom's responsibilities for Awana took her to church at least once during the week to set up for club on Friday night, and in our preschool days, she had Suzy and me in tow. Every such trip began with a stop at Miss Muriel's office. Miss Muriel was the closest Baptists get to nuns—a single lady who played the church organ for fifty-five years of Sundays and spent thirty-five of those years working during the week as church secretary.

Miss Muriel's office was upstairs near the end of the hall and next to Pastor Sawyer's dark sanctum of bookshelves and padded furniture, a place that people like me saw only on tippy-toes through a window in the door—and then only when I was sure he wasn't even in the building. Miss Muriel was the Mr. Pafford of the off-hours—a grandmotherly figure with a jar full of candy on her desk.

From Miss Muriel's office, my mom disappeared to her Awana room, and Suzy and I scattered. The church building was our playground, every door unlocked except the sound room off the sanctuary and the game room in the gym. Our adventures usually started with snack scavenging: the toddler room had graham crackers; the twos-and-threes room had flower-shaped butter cookies that fit like rings; the fours-and-fives had frosted oatmeal cookies. If we were lucky, the kitchen refrigerator might have leftovers from a youth event or ladies' lunch. We were careful to moderate our thievery, taking only a sample from each stash. There was no sense raising suspicion that might result in locked drawers or closets.

The snack rounds completed, we explored the dark hallways and back staircases, the baptistery and choir loft. If the custodian was in the building, we could get into the game room, which smelled like a box of red rubber recess balls. We hauled out enough Awana game equipment to set up two-person versions of the Friday night games: plastic bowling pins marking the giant circle, beanbags positioned for beanbag grab, Velcro straps for the three-legged race. But the best thing in the game room was the hoppity hops, the red- and blue-handled balls that we sat on to bounce the length of the gym.

Being in the church building during the week—when the lights were off and no one was home (except Miss Muriel, three pastors, and the custodian)—was like having an all-access pass. I'd been in the boiler room and the waterless baptistery. I had stood behind the pulpit, sat on the organ bench, and slipped through all the rows of the choir loft. I had seen the custodian's closet open while he did his weekly chores. I had played with Sunday toys on Thursday. I had heard Miss Muriel practice the organ on Tuesday morning. I knew where the Awana candy bars were locked up. On a really lucky day, I'd even been invited into Pastor Sawyer's office, where I confirmed with my own eyes the rumor that he had his own bathroom.

On one hand, this early familiarity bred a sense of entitlement—the building belonged to me. Subsequent years of church membership and my own involvement in ministry cemented this entitlement, such that I still feel it more than twenty years after moving away. Not too long ago, I was back in town with a friend for a wedding, and we went to church to help set up for the ceremony. When the wedding coordinator was late, I tired of waiting and went in search of the needed decorations. As I explored unlocked rooms, my friend protested that we should wait or at least get someone from the church office to help. I waved him off. This place is mine, even still.

On the other hand, knowing the ins and outs of the church bred a sense of responsibility—I belonged to the church. I knew that church on Sunday (and Wednesday and Friday) didn't just happen. It took people working there all week long to make the church building ready for the Church to show up. Church happened because there were "professionals" who saw to it that it did—people like Miss Muriel and Pastor Sawyer—and there were people like my mom and my dad. I was born into church life—almost literally.

This embeddedness in the life of the church meant its beliefs also oriented my life as surely as the physical landmarks of library and school did. Many of these beliefs were caught more than taught—such as what the role of women in the world and the church should look like. I expected to grow up and be like my mom, a stay-at-home mom who invested in the life of the church. Or like Mrs. Chandler, a children's church leader who wrote programs and skits for annual banquets, missionary conferences, and children's programs. Or like Teacher Marianne, who, best I knew, just taught toddlers in Sunday school. The women I knew were pastors' wives or missionaries' wives; they were nurses or secretaries or teachers like the Misses Carter. Some were even missionaries themselves, going to deepest Africa, like Juanita Kluve. I had every expectation I would do the same.

Other orienting beliefs were explicitly taught, like loving Jesus and obeying him, reading the Bible and praying. And I did the best I could, especially once I received my first Bible. Second graders in our church's Sunday school received their very own King James Bible on Promotion Sunday. I loved *any* new book, but the faux-leather-bound Bible was a weighty treasure in my seven-year-old hands. I recognized the gift for what it was: a rite of passage. I was old enough to have my very own Bible to read. And while I couldn't understand a lot of what was in the Bible when I was in second grade, having the book in my possession meant something. It was there to grow into, a lifelong invitation to its discovery.

I loved that Bible. And I read it, even accepting Pastor Sawyer's challenge one year to read from Genesis to Revelation during the calendar year. I slogged through a lot of it, but I did it. I underlined in it—sometimes with a straight edge (probably a church bulletin) but often not. I personalized it—with stickers that proclaimed my Baptist loyalties to Awana and with less holy stickers of fuzzy baby animals. I wrote important lists on the blank pages in the front and back—the names of the twelve disciples (twice!) and the plan of salvation (only once!). I scrawled slogans for motivation: "This book will keep you from sin or sin will keep you from this book."

My Bible went to church with me every Sunday, and when I reached junior high, I took it to school and carried it on top of my books. I loved my Bible, and I was mindful that if I was going to carry it, I needed to carry it well. I needed to love and please the God who wrote it.

I used that Bible until my parents replaced it with a burgundy leather-bound New International Version on my eighteenth birthday. Its variations of oversized crooked letters and unwieldy cursive chronicled my passage from the primary department to high school graduation. During one of those eleven years, at such a time as I'd been told that capitalizing divine pronouns showed proper respect for God, I wrote my life goal inside the front cover: "That I may KNOW Him."

I am quite sure that my understanding of this partial verse from Philippians 3 was simply this: make Jesus happy with my life. The best way I knew how to do that was to obey gladly, to be a good and faithful servant. And the best way I knew how to do *that* was not to bury my talents.

Burying my talents is an idea that comes from one of Jesus's parables in Matthew 25, on page 21 in the New Testament part of my King James Bible. With a blue pen, I marked its beginning at verse 14 and its ending on the next page at verse 30. The parable of the talents is a story Jesus told about a wealthy man heading out on an international trip. The man divides up his "talents" among his servants but not equally. He gives five to the first, two to the second, and one to the third—"to every man according to his several ability" (v. 15). While the master is gone, the servants get to work. The first two double their money, but the third "went and digged in the earth, and hid his lord's money" (v. 18). Eventually, the master returns and calls his servants to settle accounts with them. Obviously, he's very pleased by the returns of the first two: "Well done, thou good and faithful servant: thou hast been faithful over a few things, I will make thee ruler over many things: enter thou into the joy of thy lord" (vv. 21, 23).

When the third servant comes, he tells the master he was afraid and so had buried the talent. "Here, you can have it back now," he says. Sorry—"Lo, there thou hast that is thine" (v. 25).

The master is not happy and tells the servant he should have at least put the talent in the bank to earn interest. He takes it back, gives it to the servant with ten talents, and then speaks these terrifying words: "Cast ye the unprofitable servant into outer darkness: there shall be weeping and gnashing of teeth" (v. 30).

When I first heard this parable, I am quite sure it was accompanied by the explanation that a "talent" was a unit of money, like a dollar. But that fact was vastly overshadowed by the meaning of *talent* in my world. Talents were the abilities we have. It was a talent that I could read before I went to kindergarten. It was a talent that I easily finished my Awana memorization books before the year was half over. It was talent that produced exemplary report cards, glowing teacher reports, good spelling, and lightning-fast timed tests.

And while I wasn't sure what it would mean to invest such talents for the Lord, I knew that I would—and that I would reap a hundredfold and hear "Well done, good and faithful servant" on judgment day. From the time I could read that parable in my King James Bible, the driving motivation for my life was stewardship—and the fear of hearing "Cast ye the unprofitable servant into outer darkness." Not using my talents to the best of my ability in order to return more to God was unthinkable.

I don't recall anyone explicitly making the connection between this parable and God's blessing in my life, but it was certainly understood. As I grew up, I heard it in the promises given to me that God had something wonderful for my life. If I did my best to serve him, he would lead me into green pastures—a life of happy satisfaction as I used my gifts and abilities for the kingdom. It's what I lived for.

Based on the evidence around me, I believed this to be more than a hypothesis or even a theory. It was a law I could build my life on: Serve God and he will make you healthy, wealthy enough, and wise. He will give you your heart's desires—that is, he will give you the life you want. For me, that meant getting married, having a family, and serving the church.

THE TRAILHEAD

he Graduates of The Class of 1986 proudly announce their Commencement . . . as their first step forward into the future years of American History."

Since I was president of my high school senior class, I probably had something to do with this cheesy graduation announcement. Or maybe the class voted on a day I was sick. One can hope. All these years later, I wonder why some responsible adults didn't snicker to themselves and talk us out of it. I also wonder why proofreaders at Jostens didn't follow the capitalization rules of the English language.

Stepping into "American History" wasn't one of my goals in life, despite the encouragement I'd heard from more than one teacher that I could do anything I wanted to do, that I had the ability to be whatever I wanted to be. Of course, none of this was true—there were plenty of careers I was ill-suited for (being a chemist, for starters). And there were a few careers that everyone knew weren't on the list—such as being a pastor or, perhaps, being *the* president. But my teachers meant well, and besides, it didn't matter since my career aspirations didn't include any objectionable choices. I wanted to be a pastor's wife and the mother of half a dozen children, give or take.

There was one more thing I wanted to do, but I hardly dared voice it, even to myself: I wanted to be Donna Poole.

I met Donna Poole in the pages of *The Baptist Bulletin*, the flagship publication of my church's denomination, which came in the mail every month. Because I read everything in our house from cereal boxes to medical dictionaries, I read *The Baptist Bulletin* too—though somewhat selectively. I skipped or skimmed articles on Bible study or Baptist theology, lingered over human-interest stories, and read every word of the "news and noteworthy" section (with black and white pictures) at the back of the magazine. But I savored Donna Poole's column, "The Christian Woman." Donna was a thirty-something pastor's wife whose monthly column probably had as much biblical instruction as some of the articles I skipped. I read every word of her column, every month. Donna's way of writing about the Bible's intersection with daily life grabbed me, and the fact that she did it as a pastor's wife and a mother meant I could too.

Resonating with Donna Poole's writing might also be one of the reasons I wanted to be a *pastor's* wife. While there were three pastors' wives at my church when I was growing up—all quite likable—I wasn't close to any of them. Nor did I see myself in their visible ministries: Pastor Sawyer's wife was an accomplished musician, as was Pastor Smith's, and the youth pastor's wife was a nurse. But Donna Poole's gift was words, and that was something I knew.

Yes, I wanted to be Donna Poole—freelance writer, pastor's wife, mother. But not until after I went to college and, specifically, a Christian college. Besides the fact that I had grown up in a family with education and church in its DNA, I had also participated in four years' worth of youth group college tours. Each April, we spent spring break living out of the church bus as we traveled to three denominationally approved Christian colleges in our part of the Midwest. The Christian college experience, carefully curated by admissions departments, was full of fun, independence, and learning, all polished with the spiritual sheen of chapel, dorm devotions, and Bible classes. College looked like an enhanced and extended version of summer Bible camp. Bonus: each college included an expansive new library to inhabit and more classes than I could possibly take.

I decided to pursue a degree in elementary education since I considered teaching one of my talents. It also seemed like the right kind of career for the coming and going I anticipated as a wife and stay-at-home mom. The college I picked was within a day's drive of home. More important than the fact that I had scholarships there, I had a sister there. A year earlier, after spending two years working in an accounting department, Suzy had quit her job and enrolled at the small college in Ohio to work toward her own teaching degree. In the fall of 1986, my dad wedged, stuffed, and piled our college-life "essentials" in an open-bed trailer hooked up to our boat of a Buick LeSabre. He drove the harried route through Chicago and then south through a long stretch of Indiana cornfields, the rest of us praying for good weather the entire way.

Despite my excitement about college, I was nervous. While I had graduated from high school with a 4.0, the highest grade point average possible then, there had been only thirteen students in my senior class. I may have been the big-fish class president and captain of the varsity cheerleading squad, but the pond was very small. I was not sure I would swim so well somewhere else.

I gulped when I picked up my textbook for Introduction to the Humanities, whatever exactly those were, at the college bookstore. My fall course lineup also included Old Testament Survey, a freshman-required health class, and Fundamentals of Speech, a class that scared me more than anything else about going to college. I had scoured college catalogs as a high school junior in search of a school that didn't require speech class for degree completion. To my dismay, it didn't exist. Between Introduction to Humanities and speech class, I feared my college career would be short lived.

But I was determined to, as they say, give it the old college try. By the end of the first week, I had picked out my study carrel at the library and set my schedule. Every day when class ended, I made my way to the library, where I buried myself in the art and culture of the Western hemisphere until dinner. Then I'd spend the evening sitting cross-legged on my bed, surrounded by books and notebooks as I tackled the assigned reading for my other classes. I practiced speeches by talking at the cinder-block walls of my dorm room.

By midsemester, I was getting the hang of things and was even surprised to discover that the much-dreaded speech class was my favorite. This may have had something to do with the facts that Humanities took place in a darkened auditorium at 9:00 a.m., Old Testament Survey was taught by a droning professor in a large lecture hall after lunch, and the once-a-week hassle of a health class was inconveniently scheduled just before the cafeteria opened for dinner. Speech class, however, met in a well-lit classroom where I joined two dozen students whose trepidation matched my own. The young professor encouraged our camaraderie, and before too many weeks had passed, my terror had dissolved into a nervous anticipation and even thrill at the challenge of keeping an audience.

I finished that first semester with a 4.0 and a great sense of relief. I had proved to myself that I could do this college thing—at least the academic part. Classes were easy compared to the rest of campus life that I had tasted during high school college tours. I was hoping—expecting, really—to make friends quickly, to share all the great experiences a Christian college offered with a group of like-minded people. Knowing it wouldn't just happen, I had followed the frequent advice to "get involved!" First, I signed up for a team that wrote scripts for the college's traveling puppet ministry. I am a writer and I can't get enough of the Muppets (still!), so it seemed like an ideal place to find common-interest friends. Instead, I found myself among people who already seemed to be friends, and I felt out of place. The feeling never left, so I joined a different ministry team—helping with a weekly Awana club at a church an hour's drive from campus. Every Wednesday after a hurried dinner in the cafeteria, I climbed into a college van with a team of upperclassmen and a leader who flew by the seat of his pants every week, which annoyed me to no end. Strike two on finding my group of friends.

I tried again when the freshman class officers put out a call for volunteers to help with a campus-wide winter pick-me-up, a beach party in the gym. As a high school class officer, I had helped plan and execute many such events (scaled down significantly, of course), so pitching in to help with this party seemed like a good way to connect with class leaders—kindred spirits, surely. When the event coordinator called me, he asked if I would put together the photo booth, where partygoers could stand behind the prop of a goofy scene and stick their heads through cut-out holes for a Polaroid picture. I said I'd be happy to, but what I thought was, *I have no idea how to do this.* A plywood prop? Holes, cut with a saw? Paint? My handyman dad lived eight hours away, and the nodes of my friendship network on campus were few. But the coordinator left the execution of the photo booth in my solitary set of hands, as well as what I felt to be the pressure to succeed. I doubt that was intentional. He was a big man on campus by then, at least by freshman standards, and I was, well, nearly nobody. Where he might have assumed easy success, I saw only inevitable failure.

I recruited Brian, an artistic fellow freshman from my home church, to draw the design, but beyond this I do not remember anything about the "how" of this project—how I got the plywood, how I transported it anywhere (I didn't have a car), how I got holes cut in it, how I transferred Brian's design to the wood. I just remember the "where" of the work: Mr. Ramsey's barn, a mile's walk north of campus. I had not been to Mr. Ramsey's barn before, but someone who had helped assemble the class's homecoming float there in the fall must have suggested it—blue and yellow tissue paper littered the planks of the barn's upper floor. I was not part of those fall festivities, but I imagine the group that put together the homecoming float in late September had much more fun than I did, painting the plywood prop in the dead of winter by myself.

Somehow the photo booth happened, though I took little pride in the final product. Brian's design wasn't the problem; it was the head holes atop his strong man in a turn-of-the-century swimsuit and the suited woman being carried like a bride. They were awkwardly oversized, such that the photo souvenirs showed more of the bleachers behind the prop than the human heads stuck through the holes. Moreover, at least for me, the prop's allusion to fun in the sun was a mocking reminder of the lonely winter days I had spent creating it.

Maybe my friend-making skills were bad. I've always been shy—a trait I now understand to be more complex than simply trying not to be seen, hiding in the folds of my mom's skirt as a child in the church lobby. I am an introvert, but at the age of barely eighteen, I had yet to learn what that meant and how it influences the ways I interact with people. I didn't understand then that finding my people and my place, wherever I am, is more like fly-fishing in a quiet stream than trawling in an ocean.

Maybe I had a "Hey, I was a Big Fish in high school!" chip on my shoulder that put people at a distance. My freshman-year roommates would tell me much later that they felt as if they had to fight my memories to get close to me, that I kept them at a distance with my attachment to my past. But I didn't know how to live without those memories. They were the link to my identity, my sense of who I was and what I could do. They were my connection to a place and to people who knew me and loved me. Memories were both my safety net and the scaffolding that gave me the courage to climb a little higher, to venture into unfamiliar territory.

In hindsight, I can easily believe that both these things—being socially reticent and having a big-fish attitude—were true. What else was true was that I was afraid. I feared not being accepted, failing, and not measuring up to expectations—my own, others', and even what I perceived to be others' expectations.

I had two roommates that first year, and we got along well enough. Together we discovered the freshmen version of campus life, its good and bad: which professors to avoid if possible, what cafeteria meals not to miss, the best time to take Foundations of Social Science, how to manage time. We shared care packages from home and counted the days until Thanksgiving weekend.

And we laughed at the way each other talked, encountering dialect differences up close for the first time. I had a stuffed dog on my bed, a word I pronounced "dawg" to rhyme with "fog." Shelly, from north of Philadelphia, said it much like I did, though with a slightly tighter mouth. Lisa, from small-town southwestern Ohio, needed two syllables: "DOW-oog." This amused us, and Lisa's word became the stuffed animal's official name.

Shelly and Lisa were good company after a hard day, but my real lifeline was Suzy, who didn't have to fight my memories to get close. She was part of them. That year we lived in dorms separated by a parking lot and field, but from my bottom bunk next to the window, I could see her window. If the light was on in the evening, she was probably studying on her bed by her window. Home was just a short walk away. More often, she'd walk my direction, and we'd go across the street to the little grocery store to get Black Cows—chocolate-covered caramel sticks—or to the mom-and-pop ice cream shop for Tornadoes, just as good as Dairy Queen Blizzards. We didn't have a car between us until Suzy was a senior, and our small college town had few options for entertainment. We often hung out in Suzy's dorm room since her roommate was rarely there.

In spring of my freshman year, I received a summons to my speech professor's office. Since passing his class in the fall, I hadn't had any contact with him beyond smiles or small talk when our paths crossed on campus sidewalks. I had no idea why he wanted to see me, but on the designated day, I sat down in his office and waited out the chitchat. Finally, he squinted a smile, paused a maddeningly long time, and said, "Wendy, I think you should try out for forensics."

I think I laughed. By that time in my college career, I knew what forensics was, and it had nothing to do with crime scene investigations. Monday morning chapel often included an announcement by the coach of the intercollegiate speech team. He would call team members to the platform as he announced their haul of trophies from the weekend's forensics tournament and detailed how many speeches they had given (while the rest of us lazed away our weekends). His announcements always ended the same way: "These students are worthy of your applause." And we gave it. Phew.

I wouldn't have argued with his assessment. I had heard Susan Lane and Michael Schmidt do dramatic readings, perform in campus plays, and present in chapel. Their audiences didn't watch the clock.

Which is why I laughed at my speech teacher's suggestion. Sure, I aced and even enjoyed speech class, but I was no Susan Lane. I was Wendy Widder, formerly a big fish in a little pond but nothing but a minnow in the pond of my Christian college. I may have had the academic skills to research and write speeches, but I did not have the presentation skills necessary for competition. I certainly didn't have the dramatic skills to perform interpretations of literary pieces. Besides, wasn't forensics for communication arts majors?

It was definitely not a good fit, I decided on the spot. I would be content to make my platform debut on graduation day.

But as I walked back to my dorm room, I realized I had nothing to lose. If I auditioned and didn't make it, oh well. Forensics hadn't even been a word in my college vocabulary, much less in my plan. If I managed to make the team, I'd be part of a ready-made small group of potential friends—people perhaps more like me than the scriptwriters, Awana volunteers, and class officers. The forensics team was an *academic* team, and that increased my chances of finding a fit—or at least finding something better than cold afternoons by myself in Mr. Ramsey's barn.

I auditioned with a speech I had given in class and a dramatic reading from a theatrically inclined unit-mate, and I made the team. The camaraderie among the new members of the team was instant. I especially hit it off with Lana, whose smile and laugh bubbled enough for the both of us. We invented a forensics-related game to play over dinner, our version of the category of "impromptu speaking." In impromptu speaking, the judge assigns a competitor a topic and five minutes to prepare a speech, which is then delivered using minimal notes. In our dinner game, I would say something like "Friendship is like a washing machine. Go!" Then I'd sit and wait for a minute or so while her mental gears churned out a three-point response, agreeing or disagreeing with my proposition. When she was ready, she broke the silence: "Friendship is like a washing machine in three ways. First, it involves common interests. When you do laundry, you typically sort clothes into similar colors . . ." Most of our topics—and thus also responses—were ridiculous, making the game wildly fun in a nerdy sort of way.

Impromptu speaking was an entertaining dinner activity, but it wasn't one of my areas of competition. In my first semester of forensics, I entered tournaments with informative and persuasive speeches. I thrived on the research. This was long before Google or even the now ubiquitous internet, so I made friends with the reference librarian and spent Saturday mornings in the quiet library (not so quiet at other times of the week), poring over microfiche, collecting stacks of magazines and journals, and skimming armloads of books. As the data started to congeal into patterns, I crafted an outline and assembled paragraphs and sections. With the bookends of an attention-getting introduction and a bring-it-home conclusion, a speech finally emerged from my efforts. The prize was won, even without the competition.

But the competition didn't hurt any. An informative speech on McDonald's and a persuasive speech on toy safety earned me a couple trips to the platform during Monday morning chapel that fall—along with a pair of etched glass goblets, tournament trophies that I still have.

Late in the semester, the forensics coach asked if I would put together a speech for the category of "rhetorical criticism." I had no idea what rhetorical criticism was, and listening to several rounds of it at tournaments offered little help. He persisted, and I eventually agreed. Together we settled on the topic of the "Dear Abby" syndicated advice column: Why did people ask a stranger for personal advice? What contributed to the longevity and popularity of the column? What need did it meet for people? He helped me find the requisite method of analysis in academic journals known to communication arts majors, and he coached me on putting my speech together. I was the only one on the team doing rhetorical criticism that year and the next as well, when I made regular trips to the platform on Monday morning for my analysis of Gary Larson's "The Far Side" comic strip.

Forensics was a good fit. I had found my people and my place.

The coach of the team, Dr. Roberts, was an intimidating man until you knew him (and even then sometimes), but as with most of my teachers before him, he liked me, and I liked him back. He struck the balance I needed for challenge and encouragement, and I came to consider him a trusted ally and even a friend.

One afternoon I sat in his office reviewing my progress for an upcoming tournament, and as often happened, our conversation meandered into other topics. This particular day we landed in the territory of my career goals. He wasn't crazy about mine, though he didn't exactly say so. What he did was listen to me explain why I was an elementary education major (an anomaly on the forensics team) and then justify my choice with the facts that teaching was one of my gifts, I really enjoyed teaching children, and it was something I intended to do with my own kids once I left the workforce to raise a family.

He just listened, stared at me, and smirked. I stared back. He finally spoke and said I wouldn't be content with "just" that, with "just" being an elementary school teacher. Not that there's a thing in the world wrong with elementary school teachers. God knows it's a hard job and an important one. But according to Dr. Roberts, it was a job for other people. He thought I would get bored. He said I would go to graduate school for a master's degree at the very least, if not a doctorate.

"Robes," as we called him, may have been my coach and friend, but he had not known me for more than a year when we had this conversation, and his assessment of my future made me mad. I was mad at his presuming to know me better than I knew myself. And I was mad that he didn't trust me, a *sophos-moros* young adult, to know what I wanted to do.

While I'd had plenty of teachers encourage my career goals—such as they were—over the years, Dr. Roberts was the first to challenge them, to tell me that there might be something lacking in what I wanted to do. I disagreed with him. What I wanted to do was teach, but that desire was just part of the larger picture of what I believed God had put in my heart to do and what he had gifted me to do. How dare Dr. Roberts suggest that doing what God wanted wouldn't be enough!

This unsettling conversation resurfaced a few more times before I finished my college degree—a bachelor of arts in elementary education—but I shoved it in my collection of unsolicited "wisdom" from well-meaning people who loved me. Most of this collection related to the other degree I expected to get in college: my MRS. In the four years I was a college student, I had dozens of conversations in the church lobby when I was home on break, and they followed a similar script.

"It's so good to see you! When did you get home?"

"We came Friday after classes."

"How was the traffic in Chicago at that time of day?"

"Oh, like it usually is on Fridays! We didn't get home until after 9:00."

"Oh, that's Chicago for ya. When do you have to go back?"

"We have to leave after lunch."

"Oh, so soon! We sure miss seeing you around here! How are things going?"

"They're going really well. I had some hard classes last semester, but things are better so far this semester."

"That's good to hear." Three-second pause. "So, are you dating anyone?"

"Nope." Awkward smile.

Two-second pause. "Well, there's time. The right one is worth waiting for."

Still smiling. Nodding too.

"You just keep studying hard and having a good time. God will work everything out in his time."

Still smiling and nodding. "Yes, I know. Thanks."

Two-second pause. "Well, it's so good to see you. Enjoy the time with your folks and have a safe trip back!"

As a college student, I never could answer the "are you dating anyone" question affirmatively. Every February during the Sadie Hawkins week on campus, I asked either a friend or my crush of the year (which was sometimes the same person) on a date, usually a double. They always went but never asked back. Well, except for Aaron, whom everyone thought I was dating in the spring semester of our senior year. Aaron was an extroverted marketing major, and we had met during our freshman year (quite possibly through the fated beach party). He was good friends with Suzy, so we easily became friends as well. In January of our last semester, I became his go-to date. It's possible he took other girls out, but I saw no evidence of it. Really, we were dating, except for verbally acknowledging it and engaging in any displays of affection, public or private.

In all those weeks, we never talked about "us" except for a blip of a conversation driving home from a dinner date one night just before spring break. He turned down the radio and into the silence said, "I'm not sure quite how to say it, so I guess I'll just say it and tell you what I'm thinking. A lot of people have asked me what's going on between us, and I haven't known what to say. [Awkward pause.] I've really enjoyed spending time with you this semester, getting to know you . . . and I'd like to continue doing this after spring break. I'm not looking for a commitment or anything, but I'd like to get to know you better."

I didn't tell him that it was too late for that—I was already committed. What I said was a version of what he had just said—"I've really enjoyed it too" and so on. But his affirmation, such as it was, was enough for me. That is, until it wasn't anymore, which happened long before "Pomp and Circumstance" played. As I was craving more time together in the waning days of college, and eventually *any* time together, he was busy squeezing every ounce of college life out of the time he had left on campus. He had scores of friends to make memories with and countless "last time" experiences to have, but few involved me. Oh, I was there for some of them, but as a prop more than anything, a bystander watching his final hurrahs.

The day before graduation festivities began, I finally swallowed the unbelievable-to-me fact that Aaron had no plans for a "last time" outing with me. We met for lunch that day to swap pictures from the senior banquet we'd gone to (together) the weekend before. After lunch I invited him to run to town with me, but he declined. Instead, I drove him back to his dorm room and handed him his graduation gift when he got out of the car—an engraved frame with a picture of us taken during a weekend trip to Wisconsin.

It was a bitter pill. For most of that last semester, I had delighted in our growing friendship and the sweet realization that someone considered me special—at least in some way. I knew that he didn't think about our relationship in the same way I did—at least not yet—but I could live with that—at least for now. I did not want him to feel like I had robbed him of his last days of college, and I certainly didn't want him to feel pressured into a commitment. There was time for that. What I craved was the acknowledgment that I was, in fact, special; that the many months we had been each other's date mattered to him in a way his other friendships didn't. I loved him, and I needed to know whether he thought it might be possible to return that love at some point.

But he could not give me that, at least not then. I know now that he meant me no ill. He must have known that I was deeply invested, and it was surely not his fault that he meant more to me than I did to him. I suspect his near avoidance of me in the last few weeks of school was an attempt to prevent hurting me in even more ways.

After graduation we drove to different states and kept in touch until our new and separate lives consumed the time we'd once had for each other. I grieved the loss, mostly of the dreams and hopes I'd attached to him. He wouldn't have made me a pastor's wife, but he would have been a good husband and father. And that would have been okay with me. By this time in my life, I was beginning to understand that God likes to pull surprises.

THE FORK

On the evening of my college graduation, I moved back into my second-floor bedroom at my parents' house. The next morning, I went to the College & Career Sunday school class and then the worship service at the church I'd grown up in. Three weeks later, I signed a contract to teach at the same school that had launched my first steps forward into the future years of American history. Nearly everything about my life looked as it had when I had left for college four years earlier—and not at all as I had expected it to look. I had anticipated a wedding date—or at least the prospect of one—and along with that, I thought I'd be living in a different city and possibly even a different state. I expected to be preparing to teach in a new school full of new faces. Graduation felt like letting the air out of a balloon rather than sending it into the sky on its way to an exotic—or at least different—place.

Suzy, who had graduated a year earlier, was also living at home and for the same reasons: she had taken a teaching job at our K–12 Christian school alma mater, and she had debts to pay. Although the school was working to raise teacher pay, it was a slow process, and we hated to spend our meager paychecks on living expenses when Mom and Dad were willing to let us live with them for minimal room and board.

But Suzy's life had taken a monumental turn. During my last months in college, she had started dating Peter. By fall they would be engaged. When I moved back home, she was gone more than she was there, and when she was home, she wanted to be somewhere else. I was glad for the turn of events in her life, of course, but it was a double whammy for me: she was moving on without me, and I was stuck back where we'd started.

Mom and Dad were happy to have me around, and as the baby of the family, I recognized the blessing it was to have them to myself for a season. But it wasn't an easy transition for me—and perhaps for them, though they never said so. Although I had spent every summer of my college years at home, it was different being there without a fall move-out date on the calendar. I was used to the freedom of life on my own—or at least the illusion of it that living in a dorm eight hours away provided—and they were used to parenting me.

My mom lost the tidier house she'd no doubt enjoyed in my absence. My white ankle socks, half inside-out, reappeared in little piles around the first-floor living spaces, and an array of my belongings en route to my bedroom cluttered the first few steps to the second floor. We'd always set things on the steps to be taken up on the owner's next trip—or the trip after that one—but my stuff had a way of staying there longer than it should have and taking up more than its share of space.

My dad lost his parking space in the garage—by his choice, though I'm not sure he considered it a choice. He was just taking care of his little girl when he let me park my car inside and he parked outside. He waited up a little less anxiously at night knowing I would get out of my car in the safety of the garage.

I have no doubt they did their best to give me the space and independence I needed, but I think it was hard for my mom especially to understand my moodiness in those early months. She hadn't gone to college and had lived with her parents until she married my dad at age twenty-three. Besides, she never was one to cry much over the past: life moved on, and she did her best to go with it. My dad was always more perceptive and sympathetic, and I think he understood I was grieving absent friends and a lost way of life. There was no going back to the way things had been, and the way things were was not my Plan A. One afternoon not too many weeks after graduation, he tapped on my bedroom door and asked if I'd talked to my college friend Jessi yet. I told him I hadn't. He knew without me saying it that one of the reasons I hadn't called her was because it would add a long-distance bill to my room and board. Another reason, whether or not he knew it, is that I was sure we'd cry through most of the conversation (and who wants to pay a phone bill for that?). He said, "You may call her this afternoon if you'd like." He didn't have to explain. I knew there would be no long-distance bill that month.

Jessi was the first of my friends to get married after graduation, and her summer wedding in Virginia was followed by a steady stream of bridal showers, weddings, and then baby showers that continued through my twenties. A rainbow of bridesmaid dresses crowded my closet, and I gave up plenty of summer Saturdays to hear friends exchange vows—at least half a dozen of the weddings requiring weekend road trips across the Midwest. While everyone else was finding the people who would shape the rest of their lives, I was still eating dinner with Mom and Dad at the table I'd been sitting at for as long as I could remember.

Living at home got easier, and some days I even commuted to school with Dad, who had retired from his administrative career with Milwaukee Public Schools and promptly gone to work as an administrator in the Christian school we'd been connected with since I was eight years old. In the late 1970s, my parents had transferred Suzy and me from Thomas Jefferson Elementary School to a little Christian school located on the north side of Milwaukee. The school wasn't much to look at—a single-story white metal building that resembled a small warehouse. Because a far corner of the adjacent soccer field was often underwater and the rest of the field wasn't much better, the building's nickname became "the warehouse in the swamp." My parents didn't enroll us there because they were impressed with appearances. They did so because they wanted our teachers' worldviews and values to match their own.

From the beginning, my dad was friends with the superintendent, Tom Zimmerman. It wasn't a friendship built on shared hobbies such as golf or fishing—neither of which appealed much to my dad anyway. It was a friendship built on a mutual passion for Christian education generally and for our school specifically. My dad, whose day job was still with Milwaukee Public Schools at the time, jumped with both feet into the life of our tiny private school. He was willing to do whatever was needed to see the school succeed, a willingness that meant he was the one "Uncle Tom"—as we called Mr. Zimmerman in our house—phoned on a historically frigid Sunday morning one January. Pipes that ran under part of the school building were in danger of freezing. The weather was forty degrees below zero with wind chills near -80, so my dad and brother met Uncle Tom and one of the high school teachers at the school, where they shimmied through the crawl space to prevent disaster. My dad's willingness to do anything also took him to the boardroom, where he served for more than three decades—including enough years as chairman that when the school built a new conference room, they named it after him: the Doc Widder Boardroom.

I had interviewed with Mr. Zimmerman for my job at the school during spring break of my last semester in college. When it became clear to me during my senior year that Plan A wasn't going to happen, I decided that I'd rather return to the familiarity of Wisconsin than venture into the great unknown by myself. I had also interviewed with a suburban school district, hoping to create *something* new in a life that was quickly starting to look like the old. I thought the interview went well, but I never got a second call. I would eventually learn that one of God's favorite ways of directing my paths was to put impassable barricades along alternate routes.

The school had grown to nearly a thousand students by the time I interviewed, the warehouse in the swamp vacated six years earlier for much bigger facilities. So there were several elementary positions open, and I was not terribly worried about being offered one of them. Uncle Tom was always in need of good teachers, and I knew I was a good teacher who also happened to have a deep, positive history with the school. Nonetheless, I was still nervous when I sat down for my interview with Mr. Zimmerman, Superintendent. What I remember most from the interview was a strong sense of déjà vu that began when he leaned back in his chair, signature toothpick between his teeth, and just stared at me for what seemed like forever. Finally he asked, "Why do you want to teach kids?"

He wasn't looking for the obvious answer: because it's what I went to college for. He had known me since I was a shaggy-haired eight-year-old. He had been my algebra teacher during my freshman year. And he'd spent countless hours with my dad, whose spitting image I bear in appearance and temperament. I am sure I answered him by saying that teaching was something I really enjoyed, and I felt gifted and called to do it. I probably said something about the incredible influence teachers have on the next generation, blah, blah, blah.

Without a word, he held my gaze almost long enough for me to start squirming, but with unflinching composure that would have made my dad proud, I stared back. Finally he spoke and—channeling Dr. Roberts before him—told me I'd get bored in elementary school. I would realize later that, like my forensics coach, Mr. Zimmerman saw things about me that I didn't see. At the time, I was just tired of people who thought they knew more about me than I did and who suggested that what I wanted to do wouldn't be enough for me. I was frustrated that my goals didn't measure up to their expectations for me, frustrated that they thought I'd be "wasting my talents" by teaching ten-year-olds. Didn't fifth graders deserve the best teacher they could have? Didn't they deserve a smart, creative teacher?

Despite his skepticism about my long-term interest in teaching, Uncle Tom hired me. He didn't need a twenty-year commitment; he needed a full faculty for the fall. I signed on for fifth grade, a decision that popped a few buttons on my dad's shirt, and then set out to prove that teaching kids was the right job for me.

On a steamy September day just a few months later, I welcomed twenty-five squirrelly kids into my life. I quickly decided that age ten is the peak of childhood: most can tie their own shoes, get in and out of their winter wear for recess, work with a measure of independence, appreciate (for the most part) my wry humor, and all without the adverse effects of puberty.

There were the exceptionally endearing students—like Dustin Cambridge, who told me on his last day of fifth grade that he would miss me as if I "were moveing over 100,000,000 miles away. and thats a lot" (spelling never was his strongest subject). And there were students with spiritual sensitivity beyond their few years—like Donald Patterson, who slipped up to my desk one day to show me his drawing of three crosses on a hill and quietly said, "Miss Widder, Jesus must have loved us an awful lot."

Not all of my students encouraged me or gave me warm fuzzies. Some drove me insane—like Cassie Edwards, a prim and proper only child who sweetly asked me one morning if maybe her missing homework assignment was lost in the back seat of my car. (As it turned out, it was lost in her messy desk—not my messy car.) Others broke my heart—like Marcello Romano, who tried to survive his learning deficit, compounded by the wreckage of his parents' divorce-in-progress, by lying and cheating his way through fifth grade. And there were parents who tried my patience as much as their challenging children did—like Mrs. Leonard, who sent a note with her son one morning asking if I could reschedule tests on the "humongous Bible verse" and the science unit because of their busy family plans; and like the feuding split-family Wilsons, who pitted one side against the other, leaving the shambles of their son in the middle.

Fortunately, the good outweighed the bad, and each fall I eagerly set up for a fresh batch of fifth graders. I memorized names as I wrote desk tags and formatted my gradebook. I covered the walls with fresh bulletin boards and made room for fifty boxes of tissues (a standard on Christian school supply lists). Besides my students, what I loved most about the classroom was teaching the Bible. The fifth-grade curriculum worked through the Gospel of Matthew, and introducing my students to the Jesus found there—infant king, king of Israel, king of the world, king of your life?—got me up in the morning. Some days Bible class stretched into reading class. How could I do anything else in those magical moments when student interest moved beyond simply getting required information into the realm of real life, the place where *learning* connected with *living*?

My overloaded school bag made its way back and forth to school each day, most of my evenings at home filled with grading papers and planning lessons. The busy days (and nights) masked the loneliness I felt, and in my second year of teaching I was glad to make time for a new group of friends. Deb was another of the fifth-grade teachers, and her husband, Tim, also worked at the school. The two of them, along with their single friend David, and I went out together many weekend evenings, with Tim almost always picking up the tab. We often started at an Italian restaurant and ended with a round of miniature golf or a movie. Movie theaters were on the "don't" list in the church I grew up in and at the college I attended; I first stepped foot in one when Tim, Deb, David, and I went to see Disney's *Beauty and the Beast* at the Ruby Isle theater. While I was friends with other teachers and had some friends at church, Tim, Deb, and David were the first since college days who required my presence to make their group complete.

During the months we hung out, I entertained thoughts of dating David, but it was never a decision I actually had to make. He was content with our foursome equation of 2 + 1 + 1, and I was happy just to have a place to belong. Besides, I was part of the active singles ministry at church, where many of my friends were finding their spouses.

On Sundays the well-meaning church ladies continued to pat my hand and assure me that God had someone wonderful for me. I continued to nod and smile politely—and redirect the conversations. God didn't seem to be in any hurry to bring that someone along, which made it hard to see how he was going to work out his plan for my life. But I trusted him and got busy where I was, immersing myself in the singles ministry. I joined the leadership team, occasionally taught Sunday school, managed the volunteer list for Sunday morning doughnuts, and developed a weekly newsletter, distributed to the couple dozen class members on-site and mailed to those away at college. By the time the newsletter reached its 254th edition, its circulation had grown to include more than a dozen other church members who picked up their copies from my mom, stationed at the welcome kiosk every Sunday morning.

I may have lived and breathed singles ministry, but I was the exception, not the rule. It was hard to muster commitment in a class of twenty-somethings. For nine months of the year, half lived on college campuses far and near. Some returned in the summer, but even then, work schedules and family vacations resulted in limited interest and even less serious involvement. It was the same with many who lived in the area. Young adulthood is a season of exploration and path picking—career, location, relationships—trying to find a place and a people for life building. If one path seems unpromising, try another. Above all, keep your options open in case something better comes along. For our class members, options abounded at the smorgasbord of local singles ministries—where the hope was always to find a spouse and "graduate" from the singles class altogether.

I understood the impulse, but I just couldn't do it. The local church had been in my blood from the womb. I had learned, through instruction and experience, that being part of the body meant playing my part in its thriving. I had also discovered that doing so brought joy. Despite my desire to get married, I could not give my church my leftovers. I figured God was big enough to do what he wanted to do; what he asked was that I do what he wanted *me* to do. So I kept my eyes open for potential spouses, but I kept my focus on serving.

The more I did, the more I wanted to do. And the more frustrated I became with insufficient time for what was almost a part-time job (on top of teaching, which is famously more than a full-time job). My "real job" kept me from doing everything I wanted to do at church.

To make matters worse, I was getting restless in fifth grade. Bored, really, just as Uncle Tom had predicted. I grew tired of timed tests, book reports, and lists of helping verbs and prepositions—sometimes joking to friends, "I've been teaching this material for years; how do my students not know it yet?" I invented new ways to keep *my* interest. One spring a bulletin board for the oceanography unit put the entire back wall "under the sea." Then, not long after the parasite cryptosporidium had contaminated Milwaukee's water and left the entire city running for the bathroom, my class embarked on a language arts project involving the "travel bug," named "Trip-tosporidium." One class mummified a chicken I bought at the grocery store, and another did a puppet show based on *The Hobbit*. In the semester we focused on twentieth-century history, my students experienced the economics of the Roaring 20s as "employees" of Miss Widder's Hassle-Free Homework Company. They used the "cash" they earned to buy shares—and, oh, the joy of dividends! "More, Miss Widder, we'll buy more shares!" They never saw the crash coming, and some, unable to pay their desk rent, were forced to carry their books and school supplies in cardboard boxes—the closest I dared get to a Depression-era Hooverville.

Some of my colleagues enrolled in master's programs for curriculum development, special education, or reading competency. More training in education did not interest me, and my disposable income was too limited to pour into a degree I didn't care about. I kept my growing discontent to myself and tried to think of more creative projects to foist upon my class, confident that when the time was right God would make clear what was next.

Then one October afternoon in my sixth year of teaching, I went home by way of church, as I often did. After visiting with the receptionist and snacking from her stash of Swedish Fish, I headed down the hall to Miss Muriel's old office—by then the singles pastor's office.

Pastor Dan and his wife had joined the church staff while I was still in college. I first met Dan during a semester break. Rather, he met me. We crossed paths in a hallway, and where I would have shyly smiled a greeting and kept walking, he planted both feet, beamed, and stuck out his hand. "I'm Dan! We haven't met yet!"

I had expected a quick exchange; he was a busy pastor. But Pastor Dan was in no hurry. He asked about college, my studies, and my family. I soon realized that he was not just doing his pastorly duty. He was interested in me. He heard what I said like few people did. And he remembered; every time I was home after that, Dan would pick up where he had left off.

It was Dan who refused to let me drift away from my home church when I had struggled to find my place after college. But he had also made it safe for me to choose another church: "Wendy-Lady," his Peter Pan nickname for me, "you have to make a choice— the best one for you. Whatever you decide, I'm behind you."

I decided to stay. Friends like that are hard to find.

Dan became a trusted friend—a big brother, really—and valued partner in young adult ministry. We learned how to work together, making the most of his creative energy and my eye for details. He had the ideas, and I made them happen. We were a great team.

As we sat and talked that October afternoon—Columbus Day on my calendar at the time—he suddenly said, "Close the door." I did. He dropped his voice. "How committed are you to being a career educator?"

Just that morning on my drive to school, I had been telling God I was frustrated by not being able to give more time to church ministry. I desperately wanted to get out of the classroom and do church full-time.

My response to Dan's question was immediate: "Not very."

He continued, first making it clear that he wasn't making any kind of proposition. He was just speaking "hypothetically," wink, wink. He then rambled on about the expanding ministry of the church and the obvious—and not so obvious—ministry opportunities that might result.

Dan wasn't offering me a job. It wasn't within his power to do so, nor was there one currently available. He was probing my interest in full-time church ministry. Finding me receptive, even eager, he started a conversation with the staff that lasted into the spring, when I chose not to sign my teaching contract for the next year and instead took an administrative assistant position at church.

It wasn't an ideal job for my skill set, but it was what the church needed at the time. However, we were growing and on the verge of relocating to a ninety-eight-acre site. The possibilities for future service seemed endless. I just needed to get started, somewhere, and see what happened after that. More than anything, I wanted to be part of the church staff, a group committed to helping people find the best fit for their abilities. Not long before I was hired, they had encouraged one of the associate pastors to pursue a PhD and teaching career. Despite the loss of his ministry among them, they knew it was where he could best serve the kingdom. That was exactly the environment I needed.

With more than a little trepidation about the future, I notified my principal that I wouldn't be returning in the fall. Then began the difficult transition. I sorted through files, rehoming some to the other fifth-grade teachers, boxing some to keep, and filling the trash with reams of memorabilia not even a sentimental teacher needed to keep. In the last week of school, a few students stayed late to help dismantle our classroom. I invited the 153 students and their parents who had passed through my classroom door to an after-school open house and was delighted when a couple dozen bothered to come by.

The last half-day came and went too fast. It was time to say goodbye, to close a chapter without knowing what, exactly, the next chapter held. When report cards had been turned in and every classroom nook and cranny cleared of Miss Widder's stuff, I was ready to go. The building was strangely quiet and dark. There wasn't anyone around to see me leave. As I drove home, car piled high with remnants of the only job I knew—a job I knew how to do and do well—the tears started. Desperately needing a hug from someone who understood everything that was happening, I turned off the highway four exits early. Within minutes I pulled into Pastor Dan and Marcy's driveway. Marcy—also a dear friend—was home, and together we wept. I knew I was doing the right thing, but it was hard to leave something I had been so good at to begin something entirely different. And it was scary.

My job at church didn't start until September 1, and I spent the summer turning a new page. I packed away teaching materials I wanted to keep and gave away the rest to eager friends. I bought a new car, an apple-red Cavalier coupe that I would happily drive for the next fifteen years.

Something else new started to happen that summer—though it took me a while to realize because it was so unexpected. Even ridiculous.

I had met someone—or, rather, *re*met someone. Alex had appeared on the singles class roster the previous year, a fresh high school graduate. Years earlier we had ridden the school bus together—he, a kindergartener jumping from seat to seat, and I, a high schooler studying algebra. Honestly, he annoyed me to no end. By the time we encountered each other in the singles class, he had outgrown these annoyances, but I didn't give him a second glance. By age twenty-seven, I considered college "kids" my little brothers—not prospective spouses.

But I was thrilled when Alex signed up for the singles missions trip to the Atlanta Olympic Games; most people new to the class required extra encouragement to get involved. I was helping Pastor Dan organize the trip and planning to participate in it. That spring and early summer, the team met several times for training and team building. Alex surprised me. He was fun and funny, energetic and adventure loving. What really surprised me was his passion for Jesus and his heart for ministry. No one needed to convince him that being part of the church was a good thing. He was all in.

I watched him on that trip, impressed by his easy way with people. Street evangelism was not my strength by a long shot, but he thrived on engaging perfect strangers in conversation. On our long drive back to Wisconsin, the team passed the hours between Nashville and Indianapolis by reflecting on what we had seen in each other during our ten days together. Focusing on one team member at a time, we offered perspectives on one another's strengths and weaknesses, and we talked about the work we saw God doing in each of us. We told Alex he was fearless, compassionate, and good natured, gifts we wouldn't be surprised to see God use in missions or pastoral ministry.

After the Olympics, Alex joined the singles leadership team, and we spent many more hours serving together. In our common passion for ministry, we also discovered complementary differences. He was bold and assertive, while I was shy and reserved. He was confident; I was cautious. Like Pastor Dan, he had big ideas, and I was happy to help make them happen.

As much as I enjoyed his company, I didn't think he could possibly be interested in me—and I wasn't sure I could be interested in him. He was barely out of high school, and I was, well, not too far from my ten-year class reunion. But Alex had a maturity and a giftedness I hadn't seen before. And he had a deep commitment and passion for ministry.

But still. It was pretty far fetched. I enjoyed the breath of fresh air he was in my life, but I dared not think he could be, would *want* to be, more than a friend, lest I ruin the friendship we had.

Then I started my job at church, in a windowless room far removed from the main offices. Alex made a "window" for my office—an outdoor scene drawn on cardboard and covered with clear plastic, complete with a window frame and panes separated by strips of brown poster board. Whenever he was in the building—which seemed to happen often—he sauntered down the dark hallway to my office. His presence brightened it.

At the end of September, he appeared midmorning in a suit and tie, claiming to have a meeting with his boss later. He helped me stuff envelopes, and before he left he tossed something that looked like a ticket on my desk. "Hey, look what I got."

"What is it?"

"It's a ticket for lunch. Wanna go?"

I played along. "Sure!" He said he'd be back at lunchtime.

At noon he escorted me down the hall to the "restaurant," where he had set a table with a peach tablecloth, plastic plates, and blank menus. Vivaldi's *Four Seasons* played on the boom box. We sat and waited for the waiter. After twenty minutes of banter, Alex excused himself to find the waiter. He returned, having exchanged his suit coat and long tie for a bow tie. The "waiter" set down an ice-filled kettle with a two-liter of Coca-Cola and explained that Alex would be right back. Pizza and garlic bread soon appeared, the waiter disappeared, and Alex returned. So the charade went for longer than my lunch hour. Before we were finished, I knew it was time to suspend my disbelief. This really was happening. It was the craziest chapter God had started in my story yet.

THE CAVE

I was at the front end of an exciting season—a new career and ministry and a new relationship. It was an extraordinary twist on the plan God had for my life, and I was thrilled.

I joined the church staff as an administrative assistant, a newly created position on a support staff composed of two other assistants and Audrey, the near-retirement bookkeeper who kept us all in line with her cane, no-nonsense attitude, and sharp tongue. Rachel was the receptionist, leaving Kathy to juggle the needs of five full-time pastors. When I was hired, the pastors created a division of labor where Kathy and I each assisted two of them and Rachel focused on one in addition to her receptionist duties.

Because the church was growing, we were short on space. Classrooms and parking were the most pressing needs, but office space was also becoming a dire need. The building had been built thirty years earlier with four offices lining an upstairs hallway. As staff had increased, other areas were retooled or remodeled as office space. My office was in one of these reconfigured places, down a hallway kept dark much of the week. One large room had become offices for two pastors, space for an administrative assistant, and a workroom. The pastors I reported to had offices in the main hall, so my desk was outside the offices of two other pastors, and my space extended into the new workroom.

During my first few weeks of work, Kathy trained me on the database, the phone system, and other essential office tasks—like dislodging jammed paper from the bowels of the photocopier. I attended the weekly staff meeting, which quickly became the highlight of my week. The full staff—pastors, assistants, bookkeeper, and custodian—circled a large conference table, coffee and goodies in hand. We began with friendly banter, devotions, and unhurried prayer before diving into the week's issues. A stewardship campaign was in full swing, and updated blueprints for our new facilities appeared regularly. The building process was all new to me, and I took it all in. I also simply enjoyed being with these people: they were fun, and we were all working in a place I dearly loved for a cause I fully supported.

Since the division of labor was a new arrangement, my job description was a work in progress. It was also full of vague tasks—at least to me—such as "administrate all correspondence for the pastor, from dictation, computer files, or 'ghost written,' including creating a usable filing system for copies." I didn't know where to begin with this metatask, and neither did the pastors since they were accustomed to squeezing in as much of their own correspondence as they were able. Besides, it was a long walk to my office, so a lot of tasks never made it that far, leaving me to wonder which parts of "all correspondence" I should be administrating. To their credit, they always gave me the benefit of any doubts, assuming my competence and allowing me the space to figure out my way of doing things.

Having been administratively understaffed for some time, the pastors I directly assisted were thrilled at the prospect of more focused organizational help. Within my first few weeks on the job, they had each shown me the disarray their filing cabinets were in and asked me to make them functional. It was an easy enough thing to ask—and utterly within the realm of what an administrative assistant would be expected to do. It was definitely something that would help them, and I suppose it should have helped me too, giving me a window into the nitty-gritty of their ministries. But mostly what it did was overwhelm me to the point of paralysis.

I struggled to superimpose systems that would capture all the paperwork. One pastor's files included his collection of seminary notes and sermon illustrations, all of which fascinated me. I got sucked into reading everything, learning the "-ologies" of theological study and wrestling with whether an article about hell should get filed under soteriology (the doctrine of salvation) or hamartiology (the doctrine of sin). Should I photocopy it and put it in both? The other pastor's files consisted of ministry ideas, marketing brochures, and samples of resources—piles of minutiae that had no context for me. In fairness, neither pastor expected me to finish this task in the first month. They were projects I could work on as I had time—a fantastic idea in theory. In actuality, I could only see two mountains to climb, and I didn't have the right gear or enough granola to summit.

Beyond these filing projects, I floundered in the rest of my job. I simply could not find my footing, much less gain any traction. I had excelled at organizing and facilitating the singles ministry, but I knew everything about it. I lived and breathed it. Much of my new job centered around ministries I neither participated in nor knew well. Every morning I stared at a pile of what felt like miscellaneous tasks, looked "out" the window Alex had made for me, and struggled to see the big picture. When I was a teacher, every day was more or less prescribed. After the morning bell, I took attendance. We stood for the Pledge of Allegiance. Then we had Bible class, followed by reading groups. And so on, with every variation known and accounted for. If all plans failed, we went out for recess. As an administrative assistant, I had to create my own schedule, structure my own set of unfamiliar tasks on a nonexistent framework. If every plan failed, there was always filing.

There were good days, even weeks, when I thought I might get the hang of things after all. I loved the challenge of creating an information packet for newcomers. I thrived on compiling and producing the church newsletter every month. Keeping up with the growing singles ministry—and getting paid for it—was rewarding. But more often than not, I felt like the pastors were doing the really interesting work and I was just, well, assisting them, and not very well at that.

As a teacher, I had certainly known hard days—like the day a student started a fire in the bathroom downstairs. There had even been a nearly unbearable year as a teacher—with the class that stressed me into losing ten pounds. But in this new place where God had so clearly led me, the hard days were different. I called them black-cloud days, when darkness rolled in like a storm and the air was stifling. In hindsight, a better metaphor is that I felt like I was in a deep, dark hole not fit for a canary. I could not see my hand, much less God's, in front of me, and I was suffocating.

God had put me there, of that I was sure. I just didn't know why. I knew that leaving the classroom was the right decision, and I had expected a few bumps as I figured out my new job. But I was not prepared for the utter confusion and near despair I experienced on any given day.

But God had also thrown me a lifeline: Alex. After our Friday lunch at the "restaurant," Alex planned more creative lunches—a "flight" to Germany for a picnic between a castle (Fisher-Price) and a country church (from his mom's knickknack shelf); a scavenger hunt through the building; a silly quiz and a round of table tennis. He drove a motor scooter and sometimes showed up after work to take me for a ride. We started talking on the phone and snatching whatever opportunities we could find to be together. We were cohorts in the conspiracy that was our budding relationship—surprised by it ourselves and finding the secret so unbelievably delightful we couldn't quite share it yet. Besides, knowing "we" would cause a stir, Alex and I needed to be a bit surer of ourselves before we tried explaining "us" to anyone else.

That confidence came not long after a Sunday night late in the fall. After church, the singles milled about in their weekly ritual of deciding where to go out to eat. Alex and I chatted with the group until he turned to me and quietly asked if I wanted to skip the outing and go to his "secret place" instead. Brown eyes bright with mischief, he refused to tell me where it was (what's the point of a secret?). It definitely sounded more interesting than a burger at Denny's, so I agreed. We made our separate exits and sneaked to his hand-me-down family station wagon. After congratulating ourselves on a successful escape, we were on our way.

The streets we traveled were familiar to me, but when Alex finally stopped the car and turned off the ignition, I was perplexed. The deserted parking lot of a furniture store didn't seem like such an impressive secret. When I expressed my skepticism, he just smiled. We locked the car and took off walking—across the empty lot, under a spooky bridge, through a damp field, between a gap in the fence, and up a steep hill. At the top of the hill, Alex proudly presented his secret place: a bridge of railroad tracks that ran over the interstate.

For the next several hours we walked the tracks, watched the headlights zoom under us, and sat in the chilly October air, wishing upon faraway stars. And we talked. Of all the things we had discovered since returning from Atlanta months earlier, we had learned that there was never enough time to talk. Someone else always needed the phone. Classes and work ended our emails before they were finished. Responsibilities beckoned when we still had so much to say. We talked of dreams and disappointments, families and futures, successes and failures. As the moon moved across the sky, our conversation danced through the years, a slow dance that let us share and savor the memories that shaped who we were and the dreams that defined who we'd become. We were just beginning to discover the rich diversity we brought to each other. That night the hours slipped away easily—like so many before had and like so many after would.

We had, mostly, gotten over our age difference. Sure, there were plenty of challenges ahead, but neither of us questioned whether it was worth the effort.

We continued serving together in singles leadership. Alex had started an outreach ministry, a "random acts of kindness" ministry that created opportunities for meaningful conversation. During the Christmas season, our group offered free gift wrapping and hot chocolate outside a local retail store. We provided groceries, gifts, and Christmas decorations for several families in our community. In the spring we hosted free car washes. As Alex planned and participated in these events, he started feeling a pull to full-time ministry. He considered the pastorate or the mission field and was especially attracted to China. He even started learning some Mandarin words. I was excited to see his sensitivity to spiritual things shaping his career aspirations.

Because he was a college student trying to earn money for tuition, Alex drove a delivery truck to Madison and back every night, a three-hour round trip. Never a night owl, I was always in bed by 10:00 p.m. and asleep soon after. When he got home at 10:30, he'd call, and I'd gladly reach for the phone on my nightstand. We'd talk late into the night, often not hanging up until 1:00 or 2:00 a.m.—something I'd never done before and have never done since. Young love.

A frequent topic of conversation was my job and the confusion connected to it. Alex couldn't really understand how I felt. His future lay like an open road before him while mine had just hit an intense stretch of construction and a confusing detour. He listened but admitted that sometimes he was frustrated, wondering if I could do something to make the situation better. Should I start looking for another position and send out résumés? All I could tell him was "I know I'm in the right place. It doesn't make sense to me, and I don't like a lot about it. But until God uncovers a road sign pointing another direction, I don't *want* to be anywhere else." God was up to something, and I believed that in his perfect time the detour would take me somewhere.

One late night in January, Alex used the M-word for the first time: "If we were married . . ." I don't remember what followed. I was lost in the warmth and wonder of the word. Alex was neither proposing nor even thinking about it, and I didn't want him to be. He was in the middle of his freshman year of college. He had significant life decisions to make, and I wanted him to have the freedom to make them.

In the spring he exercised that freedom. The week before his twentieth birthday, he sent applications to a couple of Christian colleges—both out of state. His growing desire for future ministry had him thinking about seminary after college, and he thought a Christian college might better prepare him for that step. Accepted by both schools, he decided on the one a day's drive away.

The ramifications of his choice hit me all at once, and I was over-whelmed. I worked hard to manage the torrent of emotions, to show my support and not discourage him with my fears about the future. He affirmed his love and commitment to stay the course, and we pressed on. While he prepared to leave on a grand new adventure, I tried to figure out how to stay in the same place without him.

Then came July, the midsummer month that Midwesterners dream about in the dark cold of winter.

The month began with what amounted to a work review. I was two months shy of my first year, but the pastors had decided a sit-down was needed sooner rather than later. Pastor Dan drew the short straw, and for two days I sat in his office for a series of "Here we are after ten months" and "next level of growth" discussions. He expressed the pastors' frustration with me and my work—or lack of it. They felt like my heart wasn't in it; I was just going through the motions of my job—and not even very well. I didn't show the initiative they had hoped for. I wasn't assuming the responsibility to "make them look good." I wasn't making the necessary calls, managing their calendars, assisting with their budgets and finances, etcetera, etcetera, etcetera.

Dan was brutally honest. He asked for the same in return. I had no words while I sat in his office; in tears, mostly, while I took it all in. But I went home and did as he asked, typing up a three-page response. He was, of course, right about most things, and I told him so. My heart wasn't in my work, and I wasn't performing well. I was flailing and failing. I didn't own my job because I felt like it wasn't mine—everything I did felt like *their* job. Obviously, I hadn't yet embraced the fact that my job *was* their job; it was my responsibility to help them carry out their responsibilities as pastors.

The irony in all this is that I had wanted nothing more in life than to marry a pastor and help him fulfill his calling—whatever exactly that looked like. Yet, there I was—not a pastor's spouse but nonetheless someone whose sole job was to help pastors in their ministries. And I was utterly lost. And frustrated. I had failed, but I told Dan I didn't know how to succeed. They had assumed my ability to do the job, but I had struggled with the vague description, minimal training, and few structures.

I envied Dan and the other pastors. While they talked and strategized, studied the Bible and taught it, I shuffled their papers and tried to tie together their loose ends. I sat outside their offices and wished I could be doing what they did.

Why it took us ten months to have this heart-to-heart is anyone's guess. That we all festered in our frustrations for so long is unfortunate. I think we assumed the best of each other and then compensated when expectations weren't met. Dan admitted the whole business pointed to their own failures as bosses as much as to mine as an assistant.

So we regrouped. When they could have—perhaps should have—fired me, the pastors rearranged responsibilities, promised to provide what I needed to succeed, and affirmed their commitment to me as a staff member. I agreed to do my best, and we all agreed to do a better job of communicating.

But I was devastated. I wasn't used to not excelling, much less to failing. (How many times had I been told I could do anything I wanted to do, be anything I wanted to be?) My parents and teachers had always been pleased with my achievements and my abilities. I withered at the thought that someone—my pastors at that!—was disappointed in me.

And I was embarrassed, ashamed even. How did I not know better? Why hadn't I asked for help? Why couldn't I at least credibly fake interest in tasks I didn't enjoy—just suck it up and do the job? I expected more of myself, and it was hard to admit that I had done so poorly for so long.

I cried my way through much of the Fourth of July weekend. By midway into the next week, I finally felt as if I had two feet to stand on again. I made it through quitting time on Friday and looked forward to hanging out with Alex that weekend.

But we were struggling too. Our times together were full of tough conversations as we anticipated our impending separation. It seemed that we labored through one difficult issue, only to encounter another.

On the Sunday night two weeks after my "growth talks" at work, Alex and I ended up alone at his parents' house. We sat on separate couches in the living room and talked. I had sensed for weeks that something was going on in his head that he wasn't telling me about. I knew I had to bide my time until he was ready to talk—until he knew himself what it was and what to do about it. But that night I probed, trying to coax the issue into the open. As he stammered through his thoughts, a knot formed in my stomach.

I realized that what had hit me all at once in the spring was finally catching up with him: uncertainty about the future. He said he knew that for us to go any further meant only one thing: lifelong commitment. He wasn't afraid of that, but he also wasn't 100 percent sure of it. He was 90 percent sure, but that nagging 10 percent was giving him great angst.

Alex had always been certain. I knew when we opened the dating door that the road would be long and full of obstacles. But where I had seen obstacles, Alex had always seen opportunities.

His confidence had been contagious, helping me believe it was worth taking the chance. I didn't know what to do with his doubt. It knocked the breath—and certainty—right out of me. I told him I couldn't use the words *break up*. That was too final. Maybe *back up*? Surely 90 percent certainty was worth something.

Alex had hoped to keep his doubts to himself until he left for school, knowing that might make things easier for me; his physical absence would have been answer enough for why people didn't see us together. But it was too late for that, so he offered to keep up appearances—and I took him up on it. Anyone close to us knew what had happened, but most people didn't. I suppose it was easier to pretend, though there wasn't anything easy about it. Summer turned cold. Tears flowed. Black-cloud days got darker and rolled in unabated for the rest of the summer.

In the midst of this darkness, a good friend told me I should write a book. She wasn't the first to suggest this, but I had learned to ignore such advice. People who liked reading my short essays in church newsletters thought surely a book was in order, but I knew that putting together a page-long article on Saturday night was not the same as sustaining an idea for a hundred pages and many months. An older man at church once told me I should write a book about being single because then I'd be sure to get married. This seemed like a bad motivation to me—not to mention a twisted attempt to manipulate God. Besides, I didn't want to be an "expert" on a way of life I was hoping to leave behind.

But really, I didn't think I had a book's worth to say about anything. Several years earlier, I had attended a writer's conference on the campus of Moody Bible Institute in downtown Chicago. It was a big adventure for me, traveling by myself, navigating the perils of Chicago driving (during summer construction), and immersing myself in a new world: writing as more than a hobby. Most people at the conference were older than I was—and, I quickly discovered, most had a better idea of who they were as writers than I did.

56

After a week of sessions on using writer's guides, constructing query letters, and keeping meticulous records, I realized I wasn't ready to "Mine the Gold in Your Past," as one session had encouraged. At age twenty-three, I didn't have much past to mine, and what I did have felt more like bread dough an hour into rising—an amorphous mass of ingredients that needed more time (not to mention some intense heat) to become something useful.

I tucked my conference notes away and continued to write as I always had: journaling for myself and writing for work and church ministries and keeping up with friends. A few years later, when I was growing restless teaching fifth grade, I tested the writing waters again and took a correspondence course on writing articles for children's magazines—with, more or less, the same results.

I suppose my attitude toward "real" writing was similar to my attitude about graduate school: if the right time ever came, I would know it.

Then came Alex, the month of tears, and the right time.

An older couple from church had access to a resort ninety minutes north of Milwaukee, and they had offered its use to any staff members who were interested. Deciding that a couple days away might be good respite, I booked a two-night stay. After work one Friday in August, I followed the Lake Michigan shoreline for an hour and half to my destination, where I holed up with my Bible and journal for most of the weekend. I don't remember what my reading plan was—if I even had one. Nor do I remember where I started. But when I landed in Hebrews 11, God got my attention.

The chapter was familiar, its litany of Old Testament figures who lived "by faith" parading through the verses. I knew all their names and stories, from Abraham and Moses to the lesser-known Amram and Jochebed. But this time, I was struck by how little information they had for following God. There was no Bible, no Christian bookstore, no small group ministry. They did shockingly bold things because they simply believed what God *had* told them. Few of them saw the rewards of living righteously, but they did it anyway. They ran the race God marked out for them—in the language of Hebrews 11—because they believed life was bigger than what they could see.

I needed to hear this. More, I needed to be in their company and immerse myself in their stories, so I could better understand their remarkable faith.

I came home on Sunday afternoon with an idea and the rough outline of a book—a book about how to live the life God puts before you, the life God has called you to, no matter what it looks like. More importantly, I came home with a vision of something beyond my circumstances, something worthwhile that could emerge from my fire. That night I talked through the idea with Alex, who said, "Wendy, you can do this. You *should* do this."

I dug in. I dusted off my Bible concordance, buried myself in the Old Testament stories, and scribbled pages of notes. Weeks passed, the notes came together into outlines, and I started writing. As paragraphs became pages, I found that the study itself streamed living water through my desolate landscape, and the process of writing about what I was learning fed my soul. I spent most lunch hours pecking on my keyboard. After work and a quick dinner, I sat in front of my colossal computer monitor for the evening. I said no to extra activities and skipped impromptu outings. I had to write.

A few months into writing, the church relocated from its cramped quarters on the city's edge to ninety-eight acres of suburban dreams. The office wing was organized according to the administrative structure, so I finally shared a three-room suite with the pastors I assisted. Smiles were wide as we settled into our beautiful new home, and the energy at staff meetings was palpable. Possibilities seemed endless. Ideas floated in the air like balloons to be grabbed: soccer fields, senior-living facilities, walking paths. The winds of hope filled my sails, and I was sure that finding my ministry fit was just a matter of time.

But it didn't take long for my sails to deflate. Aside from the surroundings, my job looked the same. The new building and office arrangement hadn't changed anything. I continued to slog through each day, sitting outside the pastors' offices and wishing I could do what they did: study and teach the Bible, help people find their place in the church, and serve the needs of the congregation. I was miserable. I loved the staff, and I loved the church. But I really hated my job.

Winter turned to spring, and one afternoon when the sky stretched blue all the way to the horizon, I was summoned to a meeting in the senior pastor's office. When I arrived and saw that the two pastors for whom I worked were also there, I knew this was not a typical meeting. They did not waste any time getting to the point. When I had been hired two years earlier, we had all hoped that I would grow into the job and, eventually, find the right fit on the church staff. The first of these hopes had not happened, despite the previous summer's adjustments, and the second was irrelevant since the pressing staff need at the time was administrative assistance.

The senior pastor summed it up: "Wendy, you're not an administrative assistant. You're not happy here, doing this, and we all know it."

Clearly, I also had not improved in my ability to fake it, to suck it up and just do the work—with a smile. My coworkers knew I was unhappy, and my bosses felt bad asking me to do things they knew I didn't want to.

I still cringe at these memories. Worse than being incompetent, I was *difficult*. I was *that* employee. If they had written up a performance review, it would have read: "bad attitude, not a team player, reluctant to do work outside her comfort zone, resistant to work she doesn't like." What was I? Twelve years old and pulling a pout because things weren't going my way?

That they didn't send me home with a bank box of my belongings that afternoon was a mercy. That they gave me ninety days to find a new full-time job was a grace. That they offered to let me continue at church part-time, doing the components of my job that I really did enjoy, was grace upon grace. All of these things together were just part of why I loved them so dearly and why I had so desperately wanted to work alongside them.

I am grateful for these pastors, my friends who loved me enough to say, "Get out of here. We love you, but this is not good for you or us." I am grateful that they put up with me, that they offered their help, that they tried. I am grateful for them because, in their tough love, they freed me. When I drove home that afternoon, I was both terrified and exhilarated. I had no idea what I would be doing in ninety days, but whatever it was, it represented a step in the right direction. My friends had lifted me out of the muck and misery of the past two years. They hadn't set me on a rock—God would have to do that—but they had rescued me.

A couple of weeks before this meeting, the elementary school principal had called me. He had called the previous spring too, wondering if I wanted to come back to the classroom. I didn't. Hadn't God led me out of it? I told him no the second time as well. Then I got my ninety-day deadline. I still didn't really want to go back—wouldn't that be admitting defeat somehow? But one of the pastors encouraged me to take the job: "It's something you know you can do. Then you can take a year or two to figure things out." It was wise advice. I called the principal back.

The job was different from what I had left. I was hired as the coordinator and teacher of the school's program for academically talented students. The position played to my creative strengths. There was no prescribed curriculum, no groundwork I had to follow. My predecessor had left many of her materials, but I had free rein to do my own thing.

I embraced the challenge, structuring the four-year program on a rough framework of Western civilization. The second graders' projects revolved around Egyptian history; one week, for example, we worked with hieroglyphics. Third graders spent the year immersed in the Greek world; their favorite project was inventing (and playing) new Olympic games. Fourth graders designed cities as we worked our way through themes associated with the Roman Empire. Fifth grade projects, including constructing castle dioramas and writing fairy tales, were inspired by the Middle Ages.

I could not have asked for a better arrangement. I had students in my room for eight hours each week, and since I was considered part-time, I was not on rotations for any supervision duties such as lunch hour, recess, and bus lines. I had plenty of uninterrupted time to myself in my basement classroom, far removed from the bustle of the main hallways. I also had a computer at my desk—one of the school's first teachers with the technological luxury.

Once my planning and prep were done, I worked on my book. My hours were sufficient to qualify for health insurance, and the specialized nature of the job meant my salary was comparable to what I had made as a regular classroom teacher. With a bit of negotiation, I was able to schedule all my classes on Tuesday through Friday, leaving Mondays free for me to work at church. I still attended staff meetings, coordinated the singles ministry, and wrote the church newsletter.

By midway through that first year back in the classroom, I had finished three-quarters of my book. In my Christmas letter, I told friends the end was in sight—except for the fact that I didn't have a publisher. Did anyone have connections? A couple months later, I came home to a flashing light on the answering machine, a message from someone I'd never met—the brother of a college friend. He was an agent for Christian musicians, but he had some publishing connections. Would I be interested in letting him try to sell my book?

I couldn't believe it. In mid-July, two years after the month of tears, I cried again, this time amid laughter as I signed a contract with a publisher in Grand Rapids, Michigan. God had done what only God could do with my circumstances.

About the same time and probably not coincidentally, I had a strange feeling in my stomach. I couldn't readily identify its source— I hadn't had a bad day or week or even month. Goodness, I'd just signed a book contract! Not only did I not know what lay behind my unease, I didn't *want* to know. Life was as good as it had been for a long time. Why would I risk disturbing the peace?

I have learned that the easiest way to deal with this kind of unsettled stomach is with the Alka-Seltzer of distraction. It's a remedy I pursued many times before and after this particular day. But for reasons God only knows, that day I decided to gut it out, so to speak. I went in search of the cause.

I shake thoughts loose and clear my head best by walking, so I laced up my tennies and set out. Several blocks into my regular route, the mental debris had fallen away. I recognized what I was feeling, and I was surprised by it. It was something I'd experienced only once before in my life, several years into my career as a fifth-grade teacher: restlessness. That time, the restlessness had led to the realization that I wouldn't teach forever. Why did I feel restless now? I had the best possible job situation.

But there it was. I was restless, and this time the knowledge that followed was that August was going to be a pivotal month in my life.

I grew up in a straitlaced Baptist church. I am not given to hearing voices from heaven or reading signs in the sky. But if Gabriel himself had delivered the message to me that summer afternoon, I would not have been more certain that something was about to happen that would change the course of my life.

My first thought was that it had to do with Alex—whom I still loved and, against all logic and common sense, still hoped would find his way back to me. Two years earlier, he had left me with his 90-to-10 certainty about us—and I had clutched that 10 percent like a plank splintered off the *Titanic*. He had emailed occasionally, when, I suspected, he was homesick for the familiarity of a close friendship. When he was home on break, he sometimes called. I eventually accepted that the ratio of his certainty had shifted, and I had cut off most contact with him—for my own sake. But I still hoped. I hoped that God would surprise us again with each other.

As I reflected on what I was feeling, I was excited but scared. God had done both amazing and excruciating things to get me where I was, wherever exactly that was. I had no idea what might lay ahead. But whatever he had in store this time, I told him I was all in.

A week or so later, I was out walking again after work. As I often do when I walk, I was praying. This time, I was talking to God about several "little brothers" from the singles class who were getting ready to start seminary programs. I prayed about their decision-making, their preparation for ministry, and their futures beyond the diplomas. I asked God to do great things with them as they ventured into full-time church or missions work.

In the middle of this conversation—and what happens next assures me it was a conversation—a thought interrupted my stream of words and nearly stopped me on the sidewalk.

I wanted to go to seminary.

This wasn't the first time I'd thought about going to seminary, but every other time it was in the context of going with Alex—we would get married, he would start seminary, and I obviously would be there with him. But this time my desire wasn't appended to Alex's vocational goals. *I* wanted to go to seminary. *I* wanted to take the classes, study the Bible, and explore theology in an academic setting. *I* wanted to discover for myself what separated my office from the pastors' offices—at least in terms of education.

And why shouldn't I? True, I didn't know any women who had attended seminary, but why couldn't I?

It made perfect sense. In the months of book writing, I had finally found my voice and figured out what I wanted to write: I wanted to write material that would help people understand what the Bible says and why it matters. Savoring the learning, I had also loved the process of crafting it into words. But as I had checked off chapters on my book outline and started thinking about the possibility of publication, a sobering thought settled over me. If people actually read my book, they would likely assume I knew what I was talking about. Most would probably even believe what I said.

But why should they? Who was I to be an authority on the Bible? Sure, I had grown up in the church and gone to a Christian school for most of my life, but so had a lot of people I knew who had no business teaching the Bible. My college degree was in elementary education. Yes, it was from a Christian college, but did six Bible courses make me an expert? My training and experience could not bear the weight of responsibility I felt. I needed more education if I was going to keep writing.

It was time to get that graduate degree.

THE UNMARKED
TRAIL

*W*ithin weeks of my epiphany about seminary, I had narrowed down my options and scheduled a campus visit where several of my pastors had attended. I met with a professor who was part of the institution, having been affiliated with it for fifty years. He was highly esteemed by my pastors, and I was excited to sit where they had sat, to learn what they had learned.

Dr. MacGrath and I met in a small upstairs room of the seminary building, sunlight streaming in its single, large window. His humble, even self-deprecating, manner instantly set me at ease. He began with recollections about my pastors before moving to the obvious questions: Why did I want to attend seminary? Why did I want to attend *this* seminary? I don't remember what he actually said in response to what I told him, but I remember what I felt—perhaps because it was not a feeling I was used to, at least with people beyond my immediate family. I felt accepted and affirmed exactly as I was. Dr. MacGrath acted as if singleness were nothing out of the ordinary, and he didn't bat an eye at my interest as a woman in theology.

It's not that my friends hadn't stamped their enthusiastic approval on my thoughts of seminary or that they didn't accept or love me because I wasn't married. They were fantastic cheerleaders, wholehearted supporters of nearly everything I ever did. But for all their displays of affection, most of them assumed it was just a matter of time until I got married, until God brought that someone wonderful along. Thankfully, many had learned not to tell me this anymore, but not all. On a Sunday shortly before I left for seminary, one of the senior ladies took my hand in hers and whispered, "I'm praying for a man for you. You're too good to waste."

There was nothing of this "settling for second best" in Dr. Mac-Grath, nor was there any hand patting about the spiritual gift of singleness—another "encouragement" I'd often received. His only prayerful hope for my future was that I fall more deeply in love with God and the book he wrote.

Then he talked about himself for a few minutes. At the age when many people retire, he had changed his approach to theological study. Trained in systematic theology—studying theology by doctrine (all the "-ologies" I had learned in my filing for the pastors) and then determining what the Bible and Christian tradition have to say about each—he had grown uncomfortable with its propositional nature. The more he read the Bible (from start to finish), the more it bothered him that his approach to thinking about God didn't match God's approach to revealing himself. He was struck by the fact that the Bible is not a series of statements about God. It's not a collection of theological treatises. It is a story. God revealed himself through people and places and events, and he recorded these things in a grand story—what Dr. MacGrath called the metanarrative, the story that makes sense of all other stories.

I was hooked. Dr. MacGrath's approach, fresh at the time, and his embodiment of a lifelong student convinced me that the seminary in West Michigan was where I needed to be. I applied to the school, was accepted, and made plans to relocate the following summer. In the meantime, I continued to teach and also took seminary courses by correspondence—listening to twenty-four cassette tapes and working through a thick spiral-bound notebook for each class. I thrived on the learning and couldn't wait to jump into this new life with both feet. In August of 2000, I moved to Michigan to begin residential studies for the remaining two years of my program. Dr. MacGrath was to be my advisor.

While I was excited for what lay ahead, it wasn't easy to move. One of the pastors had told me that if I went—and he fully supported my going—I had to be willing to say I might not return. I didn't like to think that, but I knew it was possible. For the time, though, I only had to focus on going away for two years. That seemed doable. What lay beyond that was up to God. I honestly had no idea what I would do to make a living at the end of two years; I just knew going to seminary and moving to Michigan were the right things to do.

My dad rented a fifteen-passenger van, seats taken out, and on the designated Friday night, several friends from church crammed my earthly goods into it. Early the next morning our family caravan set out: Suzy drove my parents' car, along with her two young children and my mom; my brother-in-law drove the van; and I drove my little red Cavalier, my dad in the passenger seat. By midafternoon, we had reached my new apartment, where a pastor friend in the area had recruited some muscle from his church to unload the van in the ninety-degree heat. Perfect strangers cheerfully hauled my belongings to the second-floor apartment I'd be sharing with another perfect stranger, a thirty-something single woman who arrived the following week. When the van was empty, my family hightailed it to the hotel where they had reserved rooms. I met them for dinner a few hours later and then returned alone to my apartment. They had done more than enough to help and would head home first thing in the morning.

That night I sat surrounded by boxes and sobbed. The possibility of hyperventilating compounded the pitiful scene: *I don't even have a paper bag to breathe into!* My family was in a Best Western only fifteen minutes away, but they may as well have been on a different continent. I was all alone. I wanted nothing more than to repack the van and go home.

The sun came up the next day. I found the box with the coffee maker and brewed a strong cup of Gevalia, a luxury in my low-budget lifestyle. I wasn't hungry but ate a plum leftover from the previous day's travel; I would save the zucchini bread Suzy had made for me until my appetite returned. Then I unpacked some boxes, stopping often to wipe my eyes and blow my nose. Everything I touched held memories of the love I had left behind. I ironed and hung curtains my mom had made. I put up some pictures. Knowing I'd eventually be hungry again, I decided I'd better find the grocery store. I stopped at the corner gas station to get directions and then bought just enough food to get me through the next few days.

I may have felt alone that first weekend, but I wasn't. One of the reasons I had chosen the seminary was because its location felt familiar. I had relatives less than an hour away, and many people I knew from home and college days had settled in West Michigan. Over the years I had visited the area many times. With its concentration of Christian organizations—universities, seminaries, publishers, and ministry headquarters—the western side of "the Mitten State" is a mecca of Midwestern evangelicalism. It would take a little bit of time and some effort, but I was sure I would find friends and a place to belong.

Classes started two weeks later. As I walked across campus that first morning, I had no idea what I was getting into. My expectations were that seminary would affirm and add to what I already knew, like new growth on an established tree. After all, I had spent my entire life in a Christian environment: family, church, Christian school, Christian college. I had been taught the Bible from infancy, and I had been teaching it myself for many years. I knew I needed to go to seminary, but I didn't think much would change about what I already believed. The four correspondence classes I had already taken didn't affect these assumptions, and I had no reason to think residential studies would be any different.

I picked up textbooks for my first class on campus, Christian Worldview, and in the stack was a book I'd read in high school philosophy. The syllabus covered several topics that sounded familiar—deism, nihilism, existentialism, creation, fall, redemption—though a rigorous review was certainly in order. I expected a relatively easy first few weeks in that class. I was also registered for a class called Spiritual Formation, which sounded like a lightweight course to someone who grew up in the church. I foresaw a challenge in my third course, Historical Theology III: Reformation, since I didn't even know what *historical theology* meant and about all I knew of the Reformation was that Catholics weren't really saved.

My fourth class was the one I looked forward to the most—Systematic Theology I, taught by Dr. MacGrath. It met twice a week in the morning, before Dr. MacGrath's chronic fatigue wore him down each day. He used the chalkboard a little, but mostly he just talked. I'm sure he had notes, but he rarely looked at them. He taught in the same way he was learning to do theology—by story. He had written his own textbook—which was still a draft at the time, a ream and a half of photocopied paper—and he also had us reading a tome entitled *A New Systematic Theology of the Christian Faith* that proved as cumbersome to read as it was to carry.

By Wednesday night of the first week, I had been to every class once. Besides being in syllabus shock—the numbed certainty that the semester is not nearly long enough for everything in the syllabi—I was mentally exhausted. It was becoming clear that seminary was going to be more, much more than I had anticipated. By Friday afternoon I thought my head might explode. A brain bulldozer had moved in, and demolition was underway. I would never be the same.

Some of what I was learning seemed so basic, so simple, and yet I had never heard it before. How was that even possible? Had I just missed it? That was unlikely since I'd always been an excessively conscientious student. What was really happening, I came to understand, is that I had mastered the dots but they had never been connected. I had never seen the whole picture very clearly.

A pastor friend was in town one weekend not long after classes started, and we sat down to catch up. I told him I was finding the process of theological training unbelievably challenging and entirely captivating at the same time. Then I described the bulldozer in my head and said I didn't know what to do with the mess it was making of things I'd always believed. He nodded and then suggested that the bulldozer had to break up the old road in order to lay down a new one—which might end up in about the same place but with a much better foundation.

Midsemester, I had a similar conversation with my uncle and aunt who came to town to take me out for dinner. They both had been through their own graduate programs in the humanities, and they practically cheered when they heard about the bulldozer. They asked good questions and planted important seeds, all the while affirming me and the painful process I was engaging.

Despite the difficulties, there was plenty of payoff for my efforts. One of them came on a Saturday evening in September after I spent the day following Dr. MacGrath's advice. He had challenged us to read through the entire Bible fast, in as few sittings as possible. I was skeptical. His approach defied everything I'd learned about Bible study—a process of dissecting passages, focusing on specific words and concepts, cross-checking a concordance, and meditating on the meaning.

But scrupulous student and ardent admirer of Dr. MacGrath that I was, I tried it. With my cup of morning coffee, I curled up on the living room futon and read. Blasting through Genesis with relative ease, I sailed into Exodus. I got a fresh cup of coffee for the sacrificial system in Leviticus and skimmed through the wilderness wanderings in Numbers. In Deuteronomy I resisted the urge to linger over Moses's heartfelt pleas for loving obedience. By day's end I had made it through Joshua, Judges, and Ruth.

I stuck my bookmark at 1 Samuel, looked up, and admitted that Dr. MacGrath was right. My perspective on the Bible after reading that day was different from any I'd had in my life. For the first time, I felt like I might get a grip on the Story and see how all the disparate pieces fit together. I couldn't wait to finish.

Then just before the fourth week of the semester, Dr. MacGrath's aorta ruptured. Six weeks later he died, his funeral held on the election day that foisted *hanging chad* upon the American vernacular. His pinch-hit substitute was an experienced professor and well qualified to teach—but he wasn't Dr. MacGrath. He wasn't the one I had moved to Michigan to learn from. He stood behind the lectern, jingled coins in his pocket, and worked point by point through detailed notes, consolidated into PowerPoint slides that broke all the rules of font size and content length. On occasion he mentioned Dr. MacGrath's textbook, but he definitely preferred the weighty hardcover book.

Thanksgiving break came and went. I passed my final exams and returned to Wisconsin for Christmas. I was glad to be home, but I was keenly aware of how much I had changed in four short months. My family, and my dad especially, was interested in my studies—to an extent, anyway—but I could not begin to answer the onslaught of questions in the church lobby. How could I put into words what I had learned—and was learning? The lectures I had listened to and the assignments I had completed did more than add to my knowledge, though they surely did that. They also changed the way I thought, reshaped the grid through which I saw everything. And they taught me how much I didn't know. I thought I had set sail across a lake, but really, I had launched into deep waters that I didn't even know existed. The ocean was all I could see on the horizon, and there was no returning to the shore I had left. The magnitude and magnificence of the Bible surrounded me; the depths of church history and tradition extended beneath me; the vastness of the gospel stretched like a night sky overhead.

Between semesters I traveled to Israel for a three-week, on-site class in the geography and history of the Bible—the best four graduate credits I ever earned and another experience that connected dots to complete a big picture. Then I returned to Michigan for another round of classes.

During that first year I worked hard to find a new church and make it my home. But choosing a church in West Michigan is a little like selecting a toaster on Amazon: endless possibilities and a dizzying array of features. I could have visited a different church every week for my entire time in seminary. I did not have the endurance or the heart for too many months of visiting. The church was my lifeblood, a fact I knew from formal instruction and a truth I knew from personal experience. I needed to find my "foster church family" as soon as possible.

I spent much of September and October "church shopping"—a process I hated with a holy passion. Sunday plummeted from being the best day of my week to the worst. Where I used to anticipate the joyful gathering of my church family, now I dreaded walking in the doors of another unfamiliar church.

But there was no other way, so every Sunday morning I dragged myself out the door, map in hand. Once I arrived at the church du jour, I rarely took advantage of visitor parking, choosing instead to park at a distance and use the longer walk to take a few deep breaths and clear my head. Inside the building, I gathered informational materials from welcome desks, shook hands with ushers handing out bulletins, and picked a sanctuary seat with easy access to the exit doors. Then I sat and waited for the service to begin—keeping my head up, an invitation to the regulars to say hello. Sometimes they did; often they did not. Once the service started, I endured the evangelical "greet and sit" with the best smile I could muster, the worst of the service over. After the final song, I resisted the urge to duck and bolt—though most weeks it didn't matter; I could meander through the throng and get all the way to the door without anyone stopping me. Sometimes on the way home, I'd stop at the Wendy's drive-through window to get lunch as a consolation prize.

But I persisted and by midsemester had decided on a church where I had a connection to home. A Wisconsin friend attended with his wife and family, and their presence provided familiar faces and someone to sit with each week. At the time, I told a friend back home that the services were "warm and wonderful." Part of this feeling came from the music, which was primarily out of the hymnal—the songbook of my life—and accompanied by piano and organ. There was no praise team, no worship band; the simplicity was striking and, at least for me, made the selections more meaningful. The sermons were rich and stimulating, and as a seminary student, I especially appreciated their substance.

The greatest contributor to the "warm and wonderful" was the genuine affection I sensed in the congregation and among the staff members. The senior pastor had been there for twenty years and obviously loved the people—and they loved him back. It reminded me of home, where my own pastor had served for thirteen years and told the congregation frequently how much he loved us and our church, and where I weekly received hugs from members I'd known my entire life.

I did have to navigate a few significant differences in my new church. There was not a singles ministry to speak of—just a college class that was less an age-specific ministry than a holding place for young adults until they got married. At thirty-one, I was beyond a college class, and I didn't mind that there wasn't another singles class for me; what I really wanted was to be part of the whole church family. So I either attended Sunday school with my friends or ventured to an adult intergenerational class.

The church was also a bit more conservative than my home church, particularly with respect to how women could serve. At home, I'd been allowed to teach the singles class because I was under the authority of the singles pastor, a man. My new church did not allow women to teach men at all. This didn't particularly bother me, given the lack of options for singles and since I wasn't interested in teaching married men. Instead, I volunteered to teach children's weekly Sunday school and midweek programming in the summer, and I quickly got involved with the church newsletter. There were plenty of other opportunities to serve.

Despite the welcome I received from nearly everyone I met, I never did feel that I really belonged, that I was a full-fledged member of the family. I felt stuck outside the house, trying to find an unlocked door to get to where the real family was. As a single person without any family in the area, I was a square peg in a round hole.

This wasn't unique to my new church. Most unmarried people would say this is true of their church as well. But it's especially so in places like West Michigan where families run deep and wide: they have lived in the area for generations and have overachieved in fulfilling the command to "be fruitful and multiply."

The West Michigan culture has been deeply influenced and shaped by religiously conservative Dutch immigrants, their recognizable surnames everywhere: Van Andel, Veldheer, DeVos, Talsma, DeBoer. From education to the arts, health care to business, the community reflects its heritage. And, as I came to learn, these names mattered. They were connections that linked you to the family; they were your key to the house. Connections were often discovered by way of Dutch Bingo, an informal game of introductions that plays out like this:

"You're from _____? What did you say your last name is?"

"Van/van der/de-_____."

"Hmm. My college roommate was a van/van der/de-_____ from _____."

"Oh! He is my twenty-fifth cousin once-removed!"

Given long enough, it seemed that anyone with Dutch ancestry could find their room in the house. Those without the pedigree but lucky enough to have grown up in the community had a place at the table too.

My paternal grandmother was Dutch and perhaps could have played the game with success, but I had not grown up in her rural Wisconsin community. The names in her circles did not mean anything to me. Worse, I did not have the conservative-Christian hallmark of a meaningful existence: a marriage and family. The evangelical church's focus on the family left little room for me.

I don't think for a minute that any of the "deep and wide" families in my church or the larger community intentionally excluded me. Most had no idea how lonely it was to live among them. They were simply doing what solid, functional families love to do: be together. To this day, my heart both rejoices and hurts when I watch such families interact. Surely they represent precisely what God designed. Family is a beautiful thing, a gift of his good creation. But the world no longer reflects the original design of creation—there was a fall, its effects roaring endlessly like the waters of Niagara. Many, many, many of us will never enjoy the Edenic ideal of a family. What is there for us?

I wrestled with this question as I attended seminary classes that first semester. One afternoon as I sat listening to my professor in Spiritual Formation and reflecting on our readings, a wonderful convergence of theology occurred. I scribbled my thoughts about singleness in the church all over my notes. The real problem, I realized, isn't the fall; it isn't the brokenness of the world. The real problem is our failure to recognize what redemption looks like, or should look like—particularly in the relationship between singles and the church, the family of God.

By the time class was finished, I knew I had my next book. Writing while taking a full load of classes wouldn't be easy, but I had to do it. I had to do it for myself, as I found both practical application of theology I was learning and redemptive significance in the isolation I was experiencing. I squeezed out weekend hours to write, kept up with my classes, and worked part-time as a publicity assistant for a Christian publishing house. My schedule was more than full, and my brain was working overtime—a rigorous but invigorating season of life.

But no matter what project was on my desk, the mental undercurrent remained the same: What would I do to make a living when I finished my program? One possibility was to pursue a career in Christian publishing—and I certainly had a foot in that door. The flexibility of my job was ideal for me at the time, and I enjoyed my colleagues immensely, but I didn't want to work on other people's books for a living. Another career possibility was to work in some kind of church ministry, but I had no vision for what that might be—and given my most recent experience on a church staff, I was apprehensive about what such a position might look like.

Near the end of my first year of classes, one of my professors jotted a personal note at the end of an assignment I'd found particularly challenging: "You really ought to consider going on for a PhD and finding a place to teach—some place like here. . . . What do you think?"

This was a new thought. On one hand, it made all the sense in the world: teaching had long been one of my strengths. On the other hand, I had left the classroom twice already in my short career. Why should returning to teach for a third time be the long-term charm? Another significant downside was that a PhD would require many more years of school—beginning with two additional years in seminary to complete a degree that included Greek and Hebrew, required competencies for advanced biblical studies.

I was beginning to feel as if God's plan for my life was a goalpost that kept moving. First, he had led me into the elementary classroom. Then he took me out of it for church ministry. Then he introduced a potential spouse. Then he closed the church-ministry door with a fair bit of force and also removed the potential spouse. Then he brought me to seminary, in pursuit of a degree I had no idea how to use. With no marriage prospects on the horizon, I needed to be ready to support myself for the long haul. Earning a PhD would mean several more years of putting "student" in the "Your Occupation" blank of my 1040. How long could I afford to do that?

But the alternative was even less attractive. Wallowing for a lifetime in a job or career that didn't challenge me in ways I needed to be challenged or provide an outlet for my gifts was a dreadful thought. My uncle offered his advice, which included the obvious but nonetheless helpful comment: "Wendy, time is going to pass, regardless of what you choose. When it has, do you want to have the degree?"

It was clear to me that God understood and cared about me and that he had carefully directed my steps. I doubt I would have left home by myself for a four-year program, much less a PhD after that—I lacked the nerve. But there I was. I had found a home in academic work, and I didn't mind having to do it a bit longer. I switched programs and settled in for two additional years. In the meantime, I hoped something—or a significant someone—would surface that would save me the time and expense of a PhD program.

My new degree program was the master of divinity, traditionally the course of study for pastors, so there was a preponderance of men in my classes—men who were or wanted to be pastors. One might have thought this would have increased my chances for finding a spouse, but it didn't. Most of the men were either already married or fresh out of college—or both. Worse than the paucity of marriage potential was the fact that I was the odd (wo)man out—the lone female in many of my classes. I don't think any of the men minded my presence among them—and several made wonderful "brothers"—but none was in a position to be a close friend or study partner. So, while I enjoyed the academic environment, I also felt isolated in it.

This feeling of isolation was only exacerbated by those outside the seminary. When people asked what I planned to do with my master of divinity degree, they often did so with a raised eyebrow: "You're not going to be a pastor, are you?" Or "They allow women to get that degree?" A chapel speaker one day best reflected the attitude when he off-handedly commented that his message was "for all you guys going into ministry"—then he paused, suddenly realizing his audience had a number of women in it—"and for all you women going into whatever you're going into."

I may not have known "whatever you're going into" any better than the chapel speaker did, but I did know I wasn't interested in being a pastor. It did not fit my theological grid, unless I wanted to lead women or children—but even then, the title "pastor" was uncomfortable, even problematic, for me. Pastors were men, and if women fit roles that had pastoral elements, they were usually called "directors." But I'd never been a good fit for women's ministries, with their focus on wives and mothers. And I'd gotten bored, twice, teaching elementary school, so that didn't seem like my best option either. I also didn't want to oversee or direct or administrate.

What I really wanted to do was study the Bible so that I could teach it and write about it—and somehow make a living at the same time. But the women I knew who taught the Bible or wrote about it didn't have advanced degrees; they were volunteers teaching women's Bible studies or writing devotionals—like Donna Poole. I simply had no capacity to imagine a career that made use of the education I was receiving in Bible and theology. And I knew that the longer I continued on the path of higher education, the further I would remove myself from what I had always known.

But what could I do? It was the way God had taken me. There was no other way. So I kept on, trusting that he would clear enough brush from the trail for me to pick my way forward—and would be there with each step.

One of my favorite activities in those days, as I was picking my way forward, was trolling the shelves at local Christian bookstores. The publishing house Eerdmans had a small store where they offloaded their seconds and also sold an array of books from other publishers. Just a few miles from my apartment, the bookstore offered an easy escape after classes. I spent many afternoons wandering its aisles, acquainting myself with names and ideas in biblical studies. On one of my early trips, I bought a book by Marva Dawn, a name that was new to me but that occupied significant shelf space at Eerdmans. According to the book's back cover, Marva had a PhD in Christian ethics and the Scriptures from Notre Dame. My curiosity was piqued. Back home I googled enough to discover she had written a number of books and was actively involved in church ministry. Also, she had been single until she was forty. Now I was really intrigued.

When Marva gave a lecture in town some months later, I attended and listened with more than interest in her topic, which I don't even remember. I was interested in her. I squeezed into the auditorium, packed with pastors and professors, students and laity. Although Marva's name was relatively new to me, plenty of the West Michigan faithful knew it. The lights flickered to silence the audience, and after a brief introduction by the lecture coordinator, Marva made her way onto the stage. A veteran of physical suffering, she hobbled to the podium, where her face lit up with a smile. "The Lord be with you!" We heartily responded, "And also with you!"

She went on to speak for nearly forty-five minutes. Her soft, even faltering, voice belied the force of her intellect and ideas, and her winsome manner softened the indicting blows she leveled against her audience, leaders of the church. Marva loved the church—that was clear—but she had the discernment to diagnose its shortcomings and the prophetic ability to offer a way forward.

After the lecture I surveyed the literature at her resource table and read the back covers of all the titles I hadn't seen yet. My eyes locked on a phrase that described Marva's work as a bridge between the academy and the church. There it was. That was what I wanted to do. I wanted to write and teach from the wealth of the academy for the people in the pews. I wanted to enrich their knowledge and experience of God with resources they would never have access to otherwise.

This was all well and good, but I still needed to pay rent.

My dad and I talked regularly about the viability of my teaching Bible or theology in a college or seminary. Since it wasn't a church setting, neither of us had theological problems with the idea, but we wondered if other people would. I might be able to get the credentials to teach, but would I be able to get a job? I browsed university websites, surveying faculty demographics and perusing institutional preferences and policies. I talked with my professors, my pastors, and my uncle and aunt. All agreed that some schools would not hire me, but plenty probably would—and for those, the fact that I was a woman entering a field historically dominated by men might be advantageous.

I started exploring PhD programs, focusing generally on "biblical and theological studies." I didn't know which emphasis to pursue: Old Testament, New Testament, systematic theology, historical theology. I had taken classes in all of these and enjoyed them more or less equally. How would I pick?

Then one summery day at the end of my third year, I was completing my term project for Hebrew class. I had chosen to translate and analyze the prayer Hannah offered after Eli the priest told her she would have a son (1 Samuel 2). About halfway through my work, all the lights came on. I absolutely loved what I was doing. I had come to seminary because I loved the Word of God, but in that moment, I realized I also loved the *words* of God. The language of Old Testament Hebrew expressed the message of the Bible with such beautiful artistry and brought new life to familiar passages.

I finished my paper, but I didn't want to stop. I wanted to keep learning Hebrew, and I wanted to teach it. I wanted to be an Old Testament professor.

THE SWITCHBACKS

I plowed through my final year of seminary, pushing hard to complete a thesis, an internship, and the four remaining classes for my degree. I was working thirty hours a week, the magic number for health insurance benefits, and I was trying to figure out what direction to go after graduation.

My book about singles and the church came out in October. The seminary presented me with a plaque in chapel, and a group of classmates took me out for a celebratory dinner. My church in Michigan barely noticed the achievement, and I didn't make much noise about it since I didn't think I'd be allowed to sell books in the lobby anyway (a common application of the moneychangers-in-the-temple story). I compensated by making a couple weekend trips to my home church in Wisconsin, which understood the moneychangers differently and welcomed my book table.

I had settled on a PhD program at the University of Wisconsin in Madison and was accepted for the next academic year. During spring break I visited Madison to find a place to live. Through an online service of a campus ministry, I connected with a grad student who was looking to replace her roommate. Amanda invited me for lunch at her apartment, an easy twenty-minute walk from campus. A sunny upper flat with hardwood floors and white trim, it sparkled in the spring sunlight. After an amiable visit and light meal at her nicely set table, I agreed to move in.

My plan was to graduate from seminary in May, work full-time in Michigan that summer, prepare for my Hebrew studies in Madison, and continue to live in the apartment that my seminary roommate and I had shared for four years. In mid-August, I would move to Madison.

The first and last parts of this plan happened. Everything in between collapsed in an implosion that officially began a month before graduation when the university notified me and my roommate that we had to vacate our apartment by June 1. They were turning our building into undergraduate housing and needed the summer to renovate. So in the busiest weeks of the semester, Cora and I scrambled to make alternative living arrangements. She found a room with a friend, and a widowed grandmother from my church offered me her upstairs—though she told me she would be gone more than she was there; grandchildren around the country kept her plenty busy.

As I hustled to complete coursework and study for finals, I sorted out the logistics of what had become a more complicated interstate move. I could not move into my new apartment until mid-August, so the intermediate destination for my Wisconsin-bound belongings was my parents' garage ninety minutes from Madison. My brother agreed to take a load in his pickup when his family came for graduation, and a seminary friend volunteered to haul the remaining furniture on Memorial Day weekend. Other friends stored boxes until I could take them on weekend trips, and I set aside a carload with just enough to survive the summer in residential limbo.

My journal entries from those frantic weeks record the stress I was feeling. Recognizing that I needed to stem the rising tide of adrenaline in my gut, I left a message for my boss one night that

I would be late for work the next day because I needed a partial "mental health day." That night I lay awake, waves of responsibilities surging over me. I was treading water hard, and drowning seemed inevitable.

Graduation weekend was a sweet reprieve. The evening before the festivities began, I picked up my parents at the airport. On Friday morning my uncle and aunt came to town. By dinnertime my brother's family had arrived from Illinois, Suzy's family had come from Wisconsin, and college friends had driven up from Ohio. I had not expected them all to come and had been surprised when one after the other said they would. My graduation was a big deal to me, of course, and I had always assumed my parents would come. I knew my uncle and aunt would come. But it didn't cross my mind that everyone else would bother. They all had young kids, and it was inconvenient and costly to give up a spring weekend for an hour-long academic ceremony. But come they did, their presence affirming me and what I'd been up to for four years. I was honored and humbled, and I was excited for them to see my home-away-from-home.

That evening we all gathered for dinner at the home of a professor who had offered to host us. He and his wife gave me the soul-warming gift of watching my different worlds mingle. Rather than being packed around a Friday-night table in a restaurant, my guests were able to relax with one another.

I had to leave the party early for preceremony pictures, and when I arrived at the seminary, my Hebrew professor's wife was in the lobby. She handed me a card, which I thought a nice gesture: *I suppose they do this for all the Hebrew graduates. That's really kind.* I was stunned to open it later and find a generous gift inside. (Perhaps they did indeed do that for all the Hebrew graduates. It's not like I could ask any of my classmates.)

I was overwhelmed before I ever zipped up my gown or bobby-pinned my cap.

The ceremony itself only added to my emotions. The Bible faculty rewarded my academic efforts with the annual award in Hebrew studies, and I received the Dean's Award for the highest grade point average, a 4.0. On the ten-second walk across the platform to receive my diploma, I shook hands with half a dozen professors and administrators, each offering their words of congratulation. The president captured all their warm sentiments when he said, "We want you to come back here someday!" I beamed at him.

In the crowded lobby after the ceremony, graduates and guests mingled with faculty. My Hebrew professor chatted with my dad for a long time. My dad told me later, with more than a little fatherly pride, that he had called me "every professor's delight." My professor's last comment to me in the lobby that night was "Your final assignment: keep in touch."

There was great joy that weekend, but the weeks surrounding it had their share of sadness. I was sad to be leaving a familiar, safe place where so much living had happened, a place where I had grown and changed in ways I had never thought imaginable. In pastor-author Walter Wangerin's words, there were "little deaths" happening all around me as things drew to a close.[2] West Michigan may have been a lonely place to live at times, but I still had put down some tender roots there. I grieved having to tear them up.

On Monday morning after graduation, I started my summer schedule. I went to work at 6:00 a.m. and worked through lunch so I could leave at 2:00. I had set my hours with the hope of getting my forty hours and still having plenty of day left to enjoy summer and to study for fall. I may have aced my seminary Hebrew classes, but I'd learned from students in the PhD program at UW that the Hebrew there was unbelievably intense and very different from what I'd been learning. I couldn't fathom what this meant, but it terrified me. Although I was eager to get started on the last leg of my educational journey, I dreaded the long, hard road ahead. But I saw no way out. It had to be done, so I was going to do it.

By Memorial Day my roommate and I had turned in our apartment keys and resettled in the spare bedrooms we'd each been offered. I was tucked away at Gloria's farmhouse five miles north of campus, and Cora was several miles beyond that. She and I agreed to get together a couple times before I left town, but beyond that, I had few expectations. We had made good roommates, but we moved in different circles. I think we both knew, without ever saying, that we were friends for a reason and a season—both of which had come to an abrupt end, like it or not.

And I didn't like it. I felt like my home had been yanked out from under me, and with it, my sense of self. Within the span of three weeks, I had lost my cozy apartment, my roommate, my primary reason for being in Michigan, the familiarity of seminary life, and at least temporarily, most of my belongings. My ministry at church—teaching children's Sunday school—went the way of summer vacation, and my role at work downshifted with the hiring of my replacement. The feeling of security and safety that came from all these things together evaporated.

It was all so much harder than I had thought it would be. Not only was I losing the familiar; I had no idea what life would look like in Madison. I was uneasy—scared, really—about living in Wisconsin's progressive capital and attending the University of Wisconsin, a bastion of liberal education. I had last attended public school as a second grader. What did I know about all the bad things that were taught in a secular system? What if I got sucked in? What if I lost my faith? I wouldn't have been the first Christian casualty at such a place; in fact, I knew the field of biblical studies was full of scholars who had studied their way right out of Christianity. I didn't want that to be me. My defenses are always high, but they were in the stratosphere as I prepared to move to Madison.

When I talked with friends about my apprehensions and even fears about the move, I asked them to pray that I would find a church that could be my community in Madison, a place where the door was open and I would find room at the table. I didn't know how I could survive being as cut off from the warmth of a church family as I'd felt in the comfortably Christian West Michigan.

Early in June I spent a day at Mackinac Island with a friend, and we had a perfect day. As it turned out, that was my last good day of the summer. My body started to react to the grueling schedule and the stress I was feeling. In hindsight, it had been warning me for months—but even if I had realized what was happening, I don't know what I could have done to prevent it. I needed my diploma, my paychecks, and a place to sleep. I had to move somewhere by June 1 and again at summer's end. I did what I knew to do to alleviate stress. I journaled and prayed about my fears, and I talked to friends. I kept up my walking routine, and I went to bed early when I could.

I started having dizzy spells, even nausea. I was achy and ran a low fever off and on for several weeks. The doctor said it was probably a virus, but just to be sure, he sent me to a neurologist, who concluded my issues were probably inner-ear related. I missed a couple days of work and cut other days short. I felt as if I was spiraling out of control; my inner turmoil matched the scatteredness of my surroundings.

I had planned to spend the Fourth of July weekend in East Lansing with my uncle and aunt. The college town of Michigan State University is an especially fantastic place in the summer when few students are around, and we'd made a tradition of hanging out together on the midsummer holiday. We would walk the sprawling campus gardens, meander to the ice cream shop, and savor the slow pace of hot summer days at their house, where open windows were the only air conditioning. We were each other's only family in Michigan, and their home had been a regular respite during my seminary years. More importantly, they had been a wellspring of support and advice.

They were expecting me at lunchtime on Saturday, but that morning I was feeling fidgety, and my stomach was churning. I hoped an errand to the grocery store would mix things up enough to calm my nerves. I picked up a few items, checked out, and then got in line to buy stamps at the postal counter. It was a slow-moving line, and as

I stood there, adrenaline started to surge. Suddenly I was intensely hot and needed fresh air. My eyes started swimming, and fearing I'd faint, I bolted to a nearby bench and put my head between my knees. An elderly lady was also sitting on the bench. I told her I wasn't feeling well and needed to rest there for a few minutes. She smiled sympathetically and kept me company while I gathered the courage to drive the four miles back to Gloria's house.

I made it to the farmhouse, relieved that Gloria was visiting family in Colorado. I didn't know how I would have explained to her what I didn't understand myself. Besides, the last thing I wanted was for her to think that her summer boarder, a woman she barely knew, was losing it.

First, I called my uncle and told him I thought I was coming down with something and needed to cancel. This wasn't entirely true—I was pretty sure whatever was happening wasn't bacterial or viral. But I needed an explanation that would let me stay home, no further questions asked.

Then I called Cora. She had graduated with a counseling degree and had also experienced her own mental health crisis when we lived together. I needed someone who knew me to explain what was happening, to help me understand the darkness that descended around me. She came after lunch, and we talked for most of the afternoon. I told her I was frustrated that I had tried to do all the right things to manage my stress and yet had so obviously failed. I was going the only way I could see to go, pursuing God's plan carefully and wisely—and yet, here I was, coming unglued, my mind and emotions feeling as out of control as my life circumstances. Why, when I was doing my best to follow the path God had put before me, would he let this happen? I felt like he had let me down.

I was frustrated, but even more, I was afraid. Something in me had broken. *I* had broken. The person I'd always known had quit on me; my mind and body turned against me. My stomach was a twisted mass of dread. I struggled to eat anything—every bite like a cotton wad in my mouth.

That first night Cora stayed with me. She slept on the living room couch while I tried to shut out the world in my bed upstairs. I turned my back to the door, curled around my oversized Winnie the Pooh—a farewell gift from the church staff in Wisconsin—and finally fell asleep.

Dappled sunlight was streaming through the window when I awoke, the grove of trees along Gloria's driveway breaking its intensity. My stomach was already—or still—in knots. I dreaded what the day might bring, what dark emotions might overwhelm me. Cora got ready for church, prayed with me before she left, and said she'd call later.

I spent the morning praying and journaling. The what-if scenarios swirled around me. What if I couldn't pull it together? What if I had to cancel all my plans for the fall—and beyond? What if I moved to Madison and then couldn't manage the program? What if I couldn't earn enough money to support myself? What if I ended up moving back home with my parents? What if I just plain lost my mind?

When I talked to my parents that weekend, my dad recognized himself in what he heard me saying and encouraged me to make a doctor's appointment. He told me he had been to the ER three times in his life for anxiety. This was news to me, but it made his parental advice all the more valuable. He said the doctor could prescribe something to stabilize my dark mood so that I could start sorting through what was happening.

I was thirty-five, and my life had just careened off the mountain road at full speed. I felt like I was sailing over the abyss of a dark canyon. I could not see my way to survival: I was single and living on my own, and I was heading into a future that terrified me. As if that weren't enough, my ability to manage enormous amounts of responsibility had just disintegrated.

As I plummeted into despair, I quickly discovered that I was far from alone. An expansive safety net of friends spread beneath me. The hosts of my graduation party lived a couple miles from

Gloria's house and extended an open invitation to dinner; I spent many evenings in their company. New friends across town gave me a house key and dibs on their basement suite all summer long; I probably slept there more than I did at Gloria's. My friends at work rallied around me, offering listening ears, lunch outings, and walks after work. Tim and Deb, my friends from fifth-grade-teaching days, were living in Florida and bought me a plane ticket to join them on a Gulf Coast beach for a week. A friend from my home church ferried across Lake Michigan to be my travel companion on a road trip back to Wisconsin. Alex's parents—who remained my friends—wanted to break in their new trailer by moving my things to Madison, and one of my friends from work offered her company for moving weekend, including staying overnight on my first night in the new apartment.

I could not have been more loved. My family and friends were rooting for me with all their strength, and I recognized their kindnesses as gifts from God. Though he may have allowed, nay, sent me into a dark night of the soul, he had done so gently. I was grateful for his fatherly tenderness, and I took comfort in his provision of dear people who wouldn't let me go. The summer, unusually rainy that year, passed, and while I hated to leave my friends and the familiar, I was ready to get on with whatever lay ahead.

In August I moved into my Madison apartment to live with Amanda. My bedroom faced the lush backyards of a wooded parkway, and a small rickety balcony allowed me to hear the unfiltered chirping of birds and whirring of lawnmowers. Chipmunks were plentiful and easily scampered up to my balcony; I was careful to keep my screen door tightly closed with a rag stuffed in the crack along its bottom. Floor-to-ceiling windows on the south and west walls made it difficult to see my computer screen, even with the blinds closed—but I relished the sunshine. That upper flat was easily the brightest place I ever lived.

I paid half the rent but quickly discovered I did not have half the space. Amanda's furniture filled the common space, and her decor covered the walls. She never offered to make room for anything I had—which, fortunately, wasn't much at the time. What didn't fit in my bedroom stayed at my parents' house. When I asked if I could put a small table in the hallway, she told me she didn't think there was room. I never asked again. It was clear she wanted things exactly as they were—down to the crates, piles of books, and laundry baskets that littered the living room floor.

Amanda had a dining room table, but our lunch together in the spring was one of the few times I ever ate at it. When I moved in, the surface of the table had disappeared everywhere except at one end, her spot. Seated in a rolling desk chair, she both ate and worked there. Months later when I invited out-of-town friends for dinner, I gave her three weeks' notice—and still had to move the piles of mail, magazines, and shopping bags so my company could sit and eat. After my friends left and before I could even get our dinner dishes put away, Amanda had returned all her piles to the table.

I ate most of my meals at my desk. If I did eat in the living room, I sat on the couch, which Amanda had covered with a bunchy slipcover (as all slipcovers are) by the time I moved in. Mindful of her concern for the couch, I took the extra precaution of putting a blanket on top of the slipcover. I later discovered she didn't really like me (or anyone, including herself) sitting on the nearly new couch; she was afraid it would sag, like some of her friends' couches had. I suppose she allowed it because it was easier than clearing space at the table.

For the most part, I lived in my bedroom, but obviously I needed to use the kitchen and bathroom. They too were Amanda's space. One morning in the shower I counted the bottles of potions and lotions that lined the bathtub: twenty. While I dried off, I counted her toiletry items on the vanity: twenty more. I toted my toiletries in a plastic caddy like I'd used in college, and I dried my hair and did makeup in front of my bedroom mirror. In the kitchen, I washed my dishes in a plastic tub perched on the edge of the sink, which was usually full of Amanda's dirty dishes. I wiped up her messes on the countertop, blow-ups in the microwave, and crumbs on the floor.

We had agreed to alternate weeks as "the unfortunate room-mate"—the title Amanda gave to the one who had to park on the street (instead of in the one-car garage) and assume cleaning duties. She took her turns on the street, but rarely did she clean. I can tolerate an extraordinary amount of my own dirt, but—at least for me—living with other people raises the bar, if even a little. The sparkling apartment I'd visited in spring was gone when I moved in. The saint of a friend who helped me get settled that weekend cleaned the kitchen so I could unpack my things on clean surfaces, and she cleaned the bathroom just because it was so disgusting.

Amanda knew she had too much stuff and felt guilty about it—or so she said a handful of times while we lived together. Since her guilt never resulted in easier living conditions for me, I assumed her admission was more to make herself feel better than anything. I tried to give her the benefit of the doubt until one of my good friends finally said, "Wendy, she might be a nice person, but clearly, she's a bad roommate. It's okay to say it." What Amanda really wanted was not a roommate; she wanted someone to pay half the rent.

But my inhospitable environment ended at the front door. When I stepped off the porch, my new world welcomed me from every direction. Our apartment was on a main bus line to campus but a quaint street nonetheless, lined with homes that predated cookie-cutter housing. The front lawns charmed me; some had the carefully manicured look I was used to, but many more had a wild-and-free landscape: flower and vegetable gardens stretching from sidewalk to front steps. Several blocks closer to campus, small businesses had taken root—their aromas of coffee beans or Italian food wafting into the street.

To the south of our apartment was a lake, its adjoining park, and a thousand-acre arboretum—an ecological project of the university. To the north was a bike path that cut between the neighborhood's expansive backyards. It linked the southwest side of town to Camp Randall Stadium and was a main artery to campus—and yet, tucked below street level and buffered by trees and overgrown shrubbery, the path surprised with its silence. Bikers and walkers are quiet commuters.

The first morning I explored the path, I marveled at its beauty and stillness. Cool mist hung in the air, the late summer sun pushing its way above the trees. Reddening tomatoes hung heavy on the vines in yards sharing a property line with the path. Bright palettes of hollyhocks towered over bushy perennials, and black-eyed Susans were everywhere. I'd been noticing the bright yellow flowers all summer, both in Michigan and Wisconsin. Perhaps they'd always been so pervasive, but that summer of transition was the first time they caught my eye. Their dark conical centers haloed with yellow rays seemed a fitting metaphor for my life—a season of darkness encircled by delicate rays of light and, I hoped, a season of darkness from which rays of light might emerge.

After passing under a couple of pedestrian and vehicle bridges along the path that morning, I started wondering when I might actually get to Camp Randall's bustling intersection. Another bridge appeared in the distance, its arch blocking my view of the path beyond. When I got closer, the arch lifted and sky appeared in the distance. I gasped. The arch framed a view of the Capitol; its white granite dome poked above the downtown high-rises, resplendent against the blue sky.

I set my backpack down, my bottle of anti-anxiety pills tucked inside. My doctor had prescribed Lorazepam for the short term to take when the Edge felt too close. I carried the bottle everywhere but rarely opened it. Knowing I could was usually all I needed.

I was about to immerse myself in a program that made me panic, in a place I was terrified to live. And yet, the beauty around me was inescapable. God's creation, enhanced and developed by human creativity, was breathtaking. The planners and builders of Madison wouldn't have admitted it, but the physical environment they had filled and then subdued, in the language of Genesis 1, betrayed them. They reflected the image of the God who created them.

What was I afraid of? The world was God's, and everything in it—from the flaming liberals in Madison to scared little me, putting one timid foot in front of the other. Arriving at my destination seemed precariously uncertain, but the path I trod was beautiful, designed by a God who loved me deeply and lavishly.

I picked up my backpack, wrangled my arms into it, and continued to campus.

Most of my exploration that fall was on foot, supplemented with a student bus pass. I wandered along tree-lined streets, got lost in a cemetery, and delighted in the free neighborhood zoo. On campus, I discovered the shady path along the shore of Lake Mendota, scouted out the main library, and meandered through the bookstore. In the spring, I hauled out my bike and pedaled the paths that crisscrossed the city.

Unlike every other school I'd attended, the campus of UW–Madison was not clearly demarcated. The university sprawled blocks beyond its main clusters of buildings, and campus housing accommodated less than a quarter of the forty thousand students. Most, along with thousands of faculty and staff members, lived in apartments and houses scattered across the metro. Even less clear was the immaterial boundary between the university and its host city. Madison was the overflow of its academy; evidence of the university's artistic creativity and scientific discovery was everywhere.

For me, in that dark season, the city of Madison was a place that teemed with life and possibility. It set a bright backdrop against the hellish academic environment that would engulf me before the first week of classes ended.

My summer fears over the intensity of the program were justified—and then some. A class that I'd hoped to test out of (but didn't) nearly undid me. It was taught by Craig, a graduate student several years ahead of me in the Hebrew program, and I sat alongside undergraduates fulfilling their liberal arts language requirement. The handful of graduate students in the class had an additional hour of class once a week—"Fourth Hour"—and it was in that hour that I doubted every minute I'd spent in seminary Hebrew class. Craig scribbled Hebrew words on the board and asked questions that were cryptic to me: "Where did this word start? How did it become this?" My fellow grad students offered answers—some correct. I couldn't even offer incorrect answers. Craig had given us pages of charts and rules explaining the scribbles, but all they said to me was that I was a remedial student. I had no idea what was going on.

After class one day I went to photocopy the next assignment, but when I looked at what I thought I was supposed to copy, I couldn't figure out where or even what the assignment was. The book consisted of Bible-like passages—in English. That was it. No questions, no instructions. Just page after page of English texts I had read, more or less, a thousand times before.

I returned to the classroom to ask, with not a little embarrassment, what I needed to copy—and, more importantly, what I was supposed to do with it. I was horrified when Craig said I needed to translate the assigned English text into Hebrew—Hebrew composition, he called it. Anyone who has learned another language knows that translating a language you don't know into English is a far different skill than going the other direction. I'd never done Hebrew composition—nor did I have any idea how to do it.

By late September the Edge had moved uncomfortably close. One night I slogged through Craig's pages of charts and rules with a friend who was planning to start the Hebrew program the following year. She thought it wouldn't hurt to get a head start. As Samantha and I tried to make sense of words like *monophthongization* and *aphaeresis*, my adrenaline surged. Panic churned in my stomach. Minutes later, I was hunched over the porcelain bowl, staring at the contents of my dinner.

When I emerged from the bathroom, Samantha asked what she could do to help. Clearly, I needed it. I simply could not go on puking over Hebrew homework.

Samantha attended the church I had settled on in Madison. It was a smaller church and in the same conference as my home church, so it had felt familiar from my first Sunday. I recognized faces from statewide youth group events, and a couple from my home church had relocated to Madison years earlier and were members there. I had attended Wayne and Cindie's wedding as a child, and Cindie had been my Awana leader for many years. She felt like a friend. It was as close to home as I could get.

I told Samantha to call Cindie and ask if we could come over and talk.

Within the hour, the three of us were seated in Cindie's cozy family room, and I told the story of my summer—the anxiety, the panic, the Edge. My meltdown. Samantha had heard pieces of it, but it was new for Cindie. When I finished, she was teary. She hugged me hard and thanked me for sharing so vulnerably with her—for trusting her with *me*. She prayed for me—and promised she'd keep praying for me.

I needed Cindie, and I needed Samantha. Several months later, I widened the circle to include others from my new church—my pastor, my deacon, and friends from a Bible study. I asked each to "adopt me," to pray for me one day of the week. Like family, they rallied around me and eagerly agreed to help however they could. Every Sunday night I sent an email updating them on my week and how they might best pray—and every day of the week, I took comfort in the knowledge that I wasn't going it alone.

But anxiety is a multifaceted foe, and I soon realized I needed a multifaceted support system. I found a Christian counselor.

When I first met with Sara, I told her the story of why I was in Madison. When I finished, she said, "Wendy, you keep saying you have to do this program. You don't *have* to do anything. No one is holding a gun to your head."

Sara's statement seemed obvious, but overlooking the obvious is remarkably easy to do. As I sat with her words, she waited. Then she went on to say that as long as I lived in the space of "have to," I would fear failure—and fear leads to anxiety leads to panic.

"Is God so small that your life is ruined if you can't or don't get this PhD?"

Of course, the right answer was no. But I had a hard time believing it. I'd been stuck in ill-fitting jobs. They were miserable.

I went home and wrestled with what she said. I had been trying to follow God's leading—and no one was saying he hadn't led me to the PhD program in Madison—but I had also boxed him into the shape of what I considered a satisfying life. Did I believe God would still have a purpose and place for me if I flunked out of the Hebrew program—or if I chose to quit?

Sara's homework assignment was to reframe my reason for pursuing a PhD. Was I doing it because I had to or because I chose to? If I chose to do it, why? What did I believe God was calling me to do with my life, and what was my motivation for doing it?

As I journaled my way through these questions, I was able for the first time to think about my circumstances as a choice. It didn't change their difficulty, but it freed me from a self-inflicted bondage. It gave me a better reason to get out of bed in the morning than the fear of failure if I didn't.

A third facet of my support system evolved out of a drive through Chicago. During semester break, I had made a quick trip to Michigan. On my drive home, the adrenaline kicked in on the Dan Ryan Expressway. This was not abnormal—I have always hated the rush of Chicago driving—but by the time I neared the Loop, adrenaline had turned to panic. My eyes were swimming, it was hard to breathe, and I felt shaky. With one hand I rummaged behind my seat for any kind of bag to slow my breathing. I felt like I was coming unglued and knew I had to get off the road. I took the next exit and the first spot along the side street to park.

I called my parents. They agreed to meet me at a Dunkin Donuts about twenty-five minutes north of where I was. Then I called Sara's office and talked to the counselor on call. "You're going to be okay.

Breathe deeply. Open your windows. Tell me what's going on." I chattered about the side street, the traffic, and Dunkin Donuts. Hunched over in my seat, I inhaled, exhaled into the bag.

"You're okay. Just keep breathing." I did.

After my breathing had evened and my hands had steadied, I ventured back onto the interstate and conquered the distance to Dunkin Donuts. An hour later my parents arrived. My dad drove my car back to their house, and I rode with my mom. The next day they followed me to Madison and treated me to lunch. The next week, I went to the doctor and asked for a prescription.

My new church family, Sara, and Paxil were the supports that surrounded me in those tumultuous months.

I needed one more thing: to get out of Amanda's apartment.

During spring break of that first year in Madison, I pored over rental guides and a city map in search of a place I could afford to live by myself. I made appointments to see several efficiency apartments, the only option in my budget. When I stepped foot inside the door of the first place on my list, my heart sank. The entire apartment was the size of my bedroom at Amanda's. The second one was smaller. Several blocks away was a third option, where I was relieved to discover that not all efficiency apartments are created equal: this room was large enough to fit my bed, desk, kitchen table, and, if I were really lucky, a very small couch.

On Friday afternoon I checked out a fourth apartment. Its rent was slightly higher, but as soon as I walked in, I knew it would be worth every extra penny. It was newer, the paint and trim bright and fresh. Sunlight was ample, and a pass-through counter separated the kitchen from the main living space. The main room was only twelve-by-twelve feet, but by then I knew I wouldn't find anything better. I called my parents from the rental office to talk things over. They weren't home, so I left a message, resisted the impulse to sign a lease on the spot, and asked for the weekend to decide.

When I got back to Amanda's, I drew the floor plan on a sketch-pad and played with how to live in a twelve-by-twelve-foot space.

How could I fit my bed, desk, and kitchen table in that room? While I was shuffling options, the phone rang. It was my parents. I caught them up on my week of apartment hunting and concluded by telling them about the place I'd seen last. I said I intended to sign a lease on Monday.

They listened, and then my mom said she'd been checking some places online. She started to tell me about one of them. I was a little frustrated; I was the one who had spent all week looking at apartments, and I had a good idea of what was available. I was also the one who knew what my checking account looked like every month. I took a deep breath, reminding myself that she was trying to be helpful, and then went through the motions of asking how much the rent was. My mom usually talked for both of them on phone calls, but my dad spoke next. "We're intending to help so you can live somewhere where you'll be comfortable."

His words hung in the air between Milwaukee and Madison while I tried to absorb them. He went on. They wanted me to find a place where my bedroom didn't have to be the living room and where I could have friends visit and not feel squashed. For as long as I was in school in Madison, they would subsidize my rent.

When I hung up, I wept. Then I laughed. Then I did both together. My mom and dad had given me so much over the years, but this gift—this gift of a home when I so desperately needed one—was surely one of their best.

I found a one-bedroom corner apartment with plenty of sunshine, and a year after moving into Amanda's space, I gladly and gratefully left it. My deacon from church rounded up a trailer and volunteers to move my things, Suzy and Peter brought a hodgepodge of furniture from my parents' house, and I bought a couch that didn't need a slipcover.

THE FALSE PEAK

*I*n my last year of seminary, a friend had lent me a novel by one of his favorite authors, Wallace Stegner. It's the story of two couples who met at UW–Madison and forged a lifelong friendship. When career paths forced their geographical separation, they remained the best of friends, supporting each other through the ups, downs, and everything in between. They did life together.

My friend thought I might like the story because it was set in Madison—though I knew nothing of the university or Madison's geography at the time. He was right, but it also made me sad. The warmth of friendship it portrayed intensified the loneliness I'd felt in West Michigan. After three years in town, I had good friends, but none was a "do life together" friend, and I had little hope for anything better in a new place. But I bought my own copy of the book and kept it on my shelf—more a wistful gesture than anything. And in the tumult of my transition, I didn't have time to mourn the ideal the book illustrated.

I had met Samantha—whose delicious pea soup had incompatibly confronted my Hebrew homework—in Michigan when we were both on the verge of moving to Madison for the same Hebrew program. She was a recent college graduate interested in Bible translation. My Hebrew professor had introduced us, and we had gotten together a couple of times to read Hebrew. I was starting at UW in the fall, but she was getting married and planned to start the following year. Samantha and Rob arrived in Madison before I did and landed at the little church I would join a couple months later. We reconnected there and resumed reading Hebrew together every few weeks.

I met Loralee in "Fourth Hour," the class with cryptic questions about incoherent notes on the white board. She had answers—and correct ones!—to Craig's questions and even asked what sounded like intelligent questions in response. About six weeks after class started, she approached me to ask if I'd like to get together for tea and Hebrew composition. That sounded lovely—the tea, that is. And the friendship it implied.

Every week thereafter I went to Loralee's for tea, cookies, and Hebrew composition—made much less miserable by company. I offered little help for her homework and confessed one day that I was definitely getting the better end of the deal. She nibbled her cookie, made another pot of tea, and said how much she appreciated having a friend from the department to hang out with. Our male classmates, who far outnumbered us, worked together regularly, but as Loralee said, "I can't exactly ask them to come over for tea." Being women in a male-dominated department and field of study was a lonely road.

Loralee and her husband, Kyle, lived between Amanda's apartment and the coffee shop where Samantha and I met to read Hebrew. Before long she joined us. One afternoon she called to say she needed a change of scenery and was headed to the coffee shop to study. I joined her. Other days we studied together at her condo. Sometimes we splurged and went out for doughnuts.

Kyle and Rob got to know each other, and by midsemester I realized I had stumbled into a circle of friends. It was too early to know whether we were living out our own version of Stegner's novel, but the sweetness it offered was already more than I'd tasted in four years of seminary.

For the next four years, Samantha, Loralee, and I held on to each other for dear life as we navigated the perils of the Hebrew program. Our small department had only two professors, and one of them was the subject of innumerable horror stories. He issued an annual decree on the first day that if you were late for class, you were not allowed to enter until the break an hour later. It didn't matter if your bus was late ("You should take an earlier bus"), the elevators were broken (we met on the thirteenth floor), or you slipped and broke your head coming down the hall. Do not open the door. Do not knock on the door. If you were dumb enough to try either, he would tell you to leave and then make the rest of us suffer the grumpy consequences. We students had a rule never to mention a relevant book or article in class because he would assign it as course reading—without ever subtracting from the voluminous list in the syllabus. His exams always had at least one, and often several, errors. He might tell us to translate a text we had never seen, and when we'd say he hadn't assigned that text, he would say, "Oh, I didn't? Hmm. Well, it's not hard. You should be able to sightread it." For the first time in my life, I was thrilled with Bs. I'd have been thrilled with Cs if they hadn't meant academic probation.

Between semesters, Loralee, Samantha, and I scurried to get a head start on the next batch of syllabi. Where the work allowed it, we divided and conquered: each of us completed a portion of the assigned translations and its issues for class discussion, and then we shared files. We got together at Loralee's kitchen table—with plenty of tea and cookies—for long days of trudging through homework. The camaraderie eased the arduous journey.

When Samantha and Rob had a baby, she backed off her studies. Loralee and I plodded on. One summer we slogged through German class and the next summer through French to pass required competency exams. We attended academic conferences when neither our schedules nor budgets could afford it but our professors said it was "important." We showed up at countless after-hours lectures with guest speakers because it was expected. We worked hard not to attract unfavorable attention; graduate students depend on the good graces of their professors almost as much as on their academic abilities to pass.

In our third summer, Loralee and I buried ourselves in twelve-hour study days, preparing for the first battery of required exams. When we passed in August, we breathed a little easier. For the first time since starting the Hebrew program, I thought, *I'm going to make it.*

Our fourth year of classes was our last, and we finished just in time for Loralee and Kyle's firstborn to arrive. While Loralee adjusted to motherhood, I spent another long summer studying—this time for my comprehensive exams and the go-ahead to write my dissertation. When I passed, my academic status shifted to ABD—All But Dissertation. My dissertation advisor was the professor of department lore, but by that point I was fairly confident I could survive him. We had several good conversations about my topic, enough for me to know I was on the right track.

My goal was to finish as quickly as possible while also looking for a faculty position. I took out a student loan so I could research and write full-time. It was time to get on with the life God had called me to—and start contributing to my retirement account.

I kept an eye on the trickle of job postings and sent off cover letters and applications when I felt qualified (as much as any newbie ever feels qualified). Most schools will not hire candidates without their PhD in hand, but that was no reason not to apply. Obtaining a faculty position in higher education typically takes at least a year and often longer.

The process feels a bit like being on a lunar mission. You hurl the required materials into the cavernous void of cyberspace or the U.S. Postal Service, and then you wait while they make their seems-like-forever journey to and around the faraway search committee.

You rarely know where your application is in the journey—or if it even made it from one orbit to the other. You spend a lot of time "on the far side of the moon"—the zone of radio silence while a spacecraft traverses the moon's back hemisphere. Sometimes communication is not reestablished—your application careened into space. Often you receive a "we regret to inform you" letter. Rarely, you hear that your application made it through the initial rounds of sifting—and could you please send additional materials? Or meet for a preliminary interview at the annual conference? Or schedule an online interview?

If these all go well, you are invited to interview on campus. Such an invitation is extended to only two or, at most, three candidates, who each take their turn at a multiday interview. A campus visit entails teaching a class or two and interviewing with every distinguished Tom, Dick, and, in rare cases, Harriet considered relevant to the hiring process. It often involves dining with the search committee and sometimes meeting with groups of students. Then you go home, collapse in a heap, and resume waiting—this time in the radio silence of atmospheric reentry. Will your candidacy survive the intense heat or go up in flames?

The longer the silence lasts, the more likely it is that your candidacy burned up. The winning candidate gets called first, and the losers wait in interminable silence until the winner accepts the position. When the phone finally rings, the head of the search committee goes through the motions of telling you what you already know.

By the time I was entering the job market, there weren't many full-time faculty jobs available—especially in the humanities. A variety of factors in higher education had collided with economic realities created by the Great Recession, and the results were grim. They were even more bleak if you were a woman looking for a job in a Christian university, as I was. While some Christian schools were interested in diversifying their predominantly white, male faculty— or at least said they were—others were not. They couldn't legally say so, but I knew which schools were unlikely to hire me. If I didn't, browsing the school's website, starting with its faculty page, was usually quite informative. If no one on the page looked like me, it was unlikely the school wanted someone like me, and if they did, I had to think hard about what it would be like to work there. I also browsed institutional beliefs and sometimes catalogs, skimming for the code language that meant "We don't believe women should teach the Bible to men."

Still, I wasn't particularly worried. I knew God had called me, and he had always provided—no matter how bleak things looked. So when my Christian college alma mater posted a job in biblical studies, I applied with high hopes. There was only one woman teaching in the department, but I knew some of the faculty, and my sense was that they wanted more women in their ranks.

I made it through all the preliminary stages and was invited for a campus visit in December. My interviews went well. I enjoyed being back on campus, interacting with the professors, and lecturing to a room full of undergraduates. The entire experience was life-giving. I was born to be a Bible teacher. I flew home to Madison, confident I had done well.

A week passed. Then a couple more days. My phone finally rang. I was too new to the process to realize what the long wait meant.

The chairman of the search committee was gracious, almost apologetic, and gave me reasons they had hired "the other guy"—mostly, my inexperience and the fact that my diploma wasn't in hand yet.

I didn't have too much time to wallow in disappointment. I was scheduled to teach a two-week course in January for my other alma mater—the seminary in West Michigan. During my Madison years the seminary dean had kept in touch. Every so often he'd sent an email asking if I wanted to teach a summer or interim course. I had my hands full trying to pass my own classes, so I had never taken him up on the offer. But in my second year of dissertation work, I needed extra cash and experience for my résumé, so I emailed him to ask if he had anything available.

He responded quickly. One of the Old Testament professors had offered to let me have his class on the book of Daniel; he would take his wife to Mexico instead.

On a frigid Sunday morning, I left my cozy Madison apartment and drove to West Michigan, where I unpacked in a gloomy campus apartment reserved for visiting faculty. The cleaning crew hadn't done their best work—there was hair on the bathroom floor, dust bunnies scampered along the baseboards, and the kitchen counter needed a good wipe down before I'd even set my travel mug on it. The flat sheet on the double bed wasn't big enough to tuck under the mattress, and the comforter was old enough to scare me out of using it. I retrieved two blankets from the trunk of my car, packed because of the severe cold, and called Samantha's parents, who lived nearby. They brought me a fitted sheet, another blanket, a toaster, a coffee maker, and a taste of home: a bag bulging with homemade chocolate chip cookies. The apartment television didn't work, and there was no Wi-Fi, but I had cookies and coffee—I decided I would probably survive.

Fortunately, my depressing accommodations did not foreshadow the welcome I received at the seminary itself. When I showed up the next morning, the administrative assistant gave me a key, access to an unused office, and a coffee mug. I logged on to the internet, emailed Loralee and Samantha an update, and finalized preparations for my afternoon class.

For the next two weeks, I worked in "my" office, enjoyed visiting with faculty friends who stopped by, and acclimated to the seminary environment from the other side of the desk. I met friends for lunches and dinners, and I spent the weekend at the home of the professor who had hosted my graduation party.

Below the surface, a lot more was happening. Two of the seminary's Old Testament professors were approaching retirement, and I knew the administration still held the sentiments expressed at my graduation: "We want you to come back here someday!" It was one reason the dean had stayed in touch with me for six long years in Madison.

Two days before the end of my class, the dean took me to lunch. He laid his cards on the table, and in my daily report to Loralee and Samantha, I summarized what he had said: "Bottom line: the seminary will have two Old Testament openings in the next eighteen months or so. They want me, so they'd like to get me into the system, working toward one of those openings. For the other position, they'll probably do the traditional national search. However, since they'll have two openings, there's a certain sense of 'We'd like to have at least one of these be a known entity.' That's where I come in. The dean is going to put together some sort of part-time position that would give me a year or two of experience and mentorship—and time to finish my dissertation—with the goal that when the retirements occur, I would become full-time and tenure track—if everyone likes the match. He even said one of the professors is willing to give up things on his plate to ensure I have things to do and even to call it quits if necessary so I have the job."

On the one hand, I was enormously relieved by the prospect—nay, near promise—of a full-time job. I desperately wanted to get on with my life, and I had really enjoyed teaching seminary students. On the other hand, I wasn't thrilled about moving back to West Michigan. I'd had good friends during my seminary days, but it had still been a hard place to live as a single adult. To paraphrase one of my dad's favorite statements, of all the places I'd ever lived, it was one of them. But I trusted that God was in these events, and after a brief round of interviews in the spring, I notified my Madison landlords that I wouldn't be renewing my lease.

The race was on to finish in Madison. For months I had been telling my advisor that I was planning to submit my dissertation in early summer. In my end-of-semester report in May, I sent a table of contents and said I intended to be done before I moved to Michigan in July. He replied and said my work looked good.

During my two years of dissertation work, I had kept him abreast of my project, but he had not seen anything beyond my semester reports. He had indicated that he wasn't interested in seeing individual chapters; he just wanted to see the completed draft. At least that's what I understood him to say. Interpersonal communication was not one of his strongest qualities.

Near the end of June, I emailed him to ask about the format of my submission. He responded that I could just paperclip the chapter together. *Um. Okay.* I emailed back saying it was the entire draft, and I would put it in a binder for him.

The next Monday I toted my masterpiece to campus, knocked timidly on his door, and held out the binder for him. He leaned back in his chair, looked at it, looked at me, and said, "This is a chapter?" The man was impossible.

"Noooo. This is the entire draft."

"Oh," he said. "Oh. Okay. I won't have time to look at it until I get back from London"—for what I don't remember. I told him that was fine since I was getting ready for an interstate move. I left uneasily but celebrated nonetheless. That evening I started packing in earnest.

A week later I had an early morning email from him, subject line: "Need to meet." That sounded ominous. He said we needed to discuss my dissertation. That sounded more ominous. He was available that morning or later in the week. I grabbed my own binder, hustled out the door, and caught the first bus to campus. When I arrived in his office, I sat down.

He wasted no time. "This is not your dissertation."

I stared at him.

"It's not what you originally proposed, and I'm not qualified to advise it."

Silence. (Really, what can one say to that?) I waited for him to tell me the good news—or, better yet, the punchline.

What he said next I don't really remember—shock is like that. I explained to him what I had done and why I hadn't foreseen a problem. Furthermore, since I had sent him a table of contents and he hadn't waved any red flags at me, I assumed all was well.

Then I asked the fateful question, "So, what do I do?"

He again leaned back in his chair, shook his head, rubbed his eyes, and made a face as if to say, "I don't have a clue." What I think he actually said was that this had never happened to him before, and he didn't know.

I waited for him to figure it out. He finally thought his way aloud to two possibilities. I could condense my 250-page dissertation into the first chapter of a new dissertation, or I could ask the other professor to advise me instead. Option 2 would have been easy except for one small matter: the other professor had recently resigned and moved to South Africa to get married and take a teaching position there.

I said I needed to think about it. He handed me his copy of my dissertation, and I walked the long road home, carrying two copies of my masterpiece, a very heavy burden indeed. A flurry of phone calls followed, and over the next several days a number of sympathetic (and righteously outraged) friends came bearing gifts of pizza and/ or chocolate, which we devoured while we packed and piled boxes.

In the blur, I emailed the professor in South Africa—the week of her wedding—to see if she could and would help me. Within twenty-four hours she responded: "You most certainly can finish the dissertation here, and I am very happy to work with you." She said I did not need to move to South Africa; I should move to Michigan, start my job, and not worry. She would see that I finished.

I was enormously relieved but also disappointed that my degree would not come from UW–Madison. For six years I had shed blood, sweat, and tears in the Hebrew program there. I had persevered and survived, and I wanted my diploma to say as much. But I knew it was more important that I finish, and sooner rather than later. In the end, it was an easy decision. I decided to transfer and get my degree from a school I never attended.

Decision made, I turned my full attention to the task of relocation, which needed it. Ten days before my scheduled move, the company I had hired canceled my reservation. I appealed to Facebook friends for help, and a classmate from seminary messaged that if I got a U-Haul, he would come drive it. Matt and I had sat next to each other in the back row for five semesters of Hebrew. I aced our classes, and he passed them. While I had been in Madison, he had started working for the seminary, and by the time I returned, he was right-hand man to the dean. Matt joked that he'd be happy to move me back to Michigan, but he wouldn't help me move away. In other words, I'd better plan to take the job when it was officially offered.

The afternoon before moving day, I picked up the U-Haul and parked it at my apartment. The next morning I hustled to the Milwaukee lakefront where Matt arrived on the ferry. We caught up with each other on the ninety-minute drive back to Madison. A crew from my church loaded the van and cleaned my apartment. By late afternoon, Matt drove away in the U-Haul, and I went to my parents' house for the night. The next morning, I picked up my sister Suzy, and we made the trip to my new apartment, where Matt had assembled a crew of seminary students to unload most of the van. Matt's crew then took several bookshelves and two dozen boxes of books five miles farther north to my temporary office at the seminary.

The seminary had recently built a new office wing, but no offices were empty when I started. I was given the best space available, which was far removed from the hub of seminary life. There were plans to add offices to the new building, and when I came, the university president fast-tracked them because the administration wanted me to have an office with everyone else. By October the new offices—four partitioned cubicles in an interior hall—were finished. The dean's administrative assistant moved into one of them, and I was given her vacated office—even nicer than the one I'd had in January. In the dead of winter, I had overlooked the seminary parking lot; in the peak of summer, I looked out over a tree-lined walking path, the lake, and the campus bell tower in the distance. In the early mornings, I could watch the sun rise.

I did most of my class preparation in that office, where I soaked up the quiet beauty of a world I had waited so long to inhabit. I kept slippers under my desk, and my UW–Madison mug sat next to a stocked candy dish. A bright red geranium from my mom bloomed near the window. Surrounded by piles of books and reams of articles, I pecked away at lectures on my laptop. The dean was serious about making sure I had time to finish my PhD—a prerequisite for a full-time position—so in my two years in the position he had created, I only had three courses to prepare; each semester I taught two of them.

I used the community refrigerator in the break room for my lunches, but it started getting crowded. This posed no problem for the majority of faculty and staff who had minifridges in their offices. One day while I was wedging my food into the fridge, I muttered to Matt nearby that I needed a fridge in my office.

"Ask Alicia," he said. Alicia was the dean's administrative assistant.

"I don't really have much clout around here to just ask for a fridge. I'm a part-time, nontenure-track, visiting professor without my PhD."

Two days later, I was copied on an email from the dean to Alicia that she should order a fridge for me. Matt, I learned, had gone straight to his office after our conversation and sent the dean an email about getting more faculty fridges. The dean replied that they'd take inventory after the school year and order for new faculty then.

Matt emailed him back: "This is for *Wendy*. She needs a fridge."

I had a fridge within a week.

My office door was usually propped open. Faculty and staff friends stopped in to chat, and those I didn't know introduced themselves. When the university president, a Bears fan, happened to be in the building, he'd stick his head in to check on the resident Cheesehead. Women who were enrolled in Bible programs appeared in my doorway regularly. Their enthusiasm and even relief that a woman was finally on faculty encouraged me, and at Christmastime I invited all the women pursing Bible degrees to my apartment. I hoped they would get to know each other and find a friend in me as well. A light snow on the day of the party kept most of them home, but the two who came stayed late into the night. I initiated several more gatherings, glad to see the women finding like-minded—and like-gendered—friends in their field.

My office was sandwiched between those of the two retiring Old Testament professors. One of them passed my office on the way to his, and he sometimes stopped to exchange pleasantries. He hadn't taught any of my classes when I was a student, but he and his wife had led the three-week trip to Israel during my first year. Since all the courses the dean assigned to me had been his, he gave me CDs with his PowerPoint presentations to use or adapt, and when he started to whittle down his library, he gave me first dibs—anything I wanted for free.

A handful of times early on, the other Old Testament professor—my Hebrew professor—paused in my open doorway if he happened to be coming back from the break room. He never said much, which was his style. But I realized after a while that I wasn't sure he was glad to have me back. This thought surprised me—why wouldn't he be happy, even gratified, to have one of his star pupils following in his footsteps? He had affirmed me as a student, and I had even chosen the program in Madison at his recommendation. I had expected a warm welcome—at least as warm as my send-off six years earlier had been. Since I couldn't come up with any reason why he wouldn't be happy with me, I told myself he must be.

Peer reviews were a regular part of faculty assessment, typically carried out on a rotation. For me, during three consecutive semesters, the dean and three members of the Bible faculty observed and evaluated my teaching. The dean compiled their feedback into detailed reports for my faculty file. The reports were overwhelmingly positive, though they included constructive criticism as well. One professor said I should use more PowerPoint and less whiteboard. Another suggested I incorporate more time for in-class reflection on ministry application. A third pointed out a better textbook for my syllabus.

When the dean had proposed the position to me, he had said it would provide mentorship. I suspect the peer reviews were part of this mentorship, but I had hoped for more from total immersion in the department. I had thought that the Old Testament professors would take me under their wings and offer some of their wisdom. They had years of experience in the biblical text, in the seminary classroom, and in the field of Old Testament scholarship. Already in my forties, I was coming into the field a good ten years after most new professors, and I had no idea how to catch up. I desperately wanted help, but I didn't know how to ask.

The absence of personal mentorship would have simply been disappointing if, shortly after my first Christmas back at the seminary, I hadn't started to sense that the hiring game had changed. What the dean had practically promised me seemed not to be the way things were going to happen.

My suspicions were confirmed when the seminary launched its search for two Old Testament professors in the spring. I was invited to apply. My faculty friends unanimously declared that I had nothing to worry about. My classes were going well, my peer reviews were solid, and I was an award-winning alum who would be a great asset to the school. They considered the process a formality—and I did my best to believe them.

But the ground under my feet had shifted. I wasn't just there gaining experience and building relationships. I was a candidate, every day of the week, until the search committee would make its decision eighteen months after I had returned to Michigan.

The committee consisted of three members of the Bible faculty— the two retiring Old Testament professors and a New Testament professor. The dean oversaw the committee's efforts, and since he had spearheaded my return to the seminary, I felt as if he was in my corner. I also knew the New Testament professor wholeheartedly supported my hiring. But I had lost confidence that the Old Testament professors were interested in seeing me step into their almost-empty shoes—a turn of events that paralyzed me as much as it perplexed me. What had I done wrong? What was I doing wrong?

As the months wore on, the field of candidates narrowed. I survived all the cuts. I also longed for the days of lunar-mission job applications when I waited in unknowing silence. At the seminary, my office was directly across the hall from the conference room where the search committee hunkered down for hours. I started keeping my door closed. When they selected the candidates for campus interviews, I knew every finalist's name and credentials. For weeks I endured the parade of my competitors on campus. One of my faculty friends said it was like watching my parents bring in other children to replace me.

The faculty was rooting for me, none of them really believing I wouldn't get the job, and all of them were committed to encouraging me through the excruciating process. Matt was one of the most vocal. One day when I moaned that I felt like I'd been candidating forever and still had months to go, he said I should think of it more as a courtship than a candidacy. I told him that probably wasn't the best metaphor to use with me, his forty-something single friend. He countered, "Yeah, but have you ever been in a courtship relationship where you were given a refrigerator, and then things didn't work out? See, this is going to break the pattern!"

I was charmed by his logic but unconvinced.

Days before my official campus interview, and barely a day too soon, I received notification from my dissertation advisor that I had passed: my PhD was completed. I had also recently signed a contract to write a volume for a Bible commentary series, a noteworthy achievement on my résumé. For my faculty friends, the victory lap had nearly begun.

On the appointed Thursday, I made my way to campus for my first interview, which was with the university president. He had interviewed me two years earlier, so rather than asking typical questions for a potential hire, he assumed a pastoral role. How was I doing, and what would I do if I didn't get the position? I was surprised by his questions, but I responded honestly. With a few tears, I told my pastor-president about the difficulties of being a candidate for eighteen months, and I told him I had no Plan B. He asked where I saw myself in five or ten years, and I said, "Here, I hope." We ended our interview talking about *Downton Abbey* and *Lost*. Then he prayed for me and sent me on my way.

I returned to the seminary for a "get to know you" interview with a group of students before having lunch with the search committee, our only meeting during my campus interview. It was the event I dreaded most. I did not want to spend an hour trying to say the right things to the group that had stopped feeling safe months earlier. I was keenly aware that I had the most to lose of all the candidates. If they didn't get the job, they stayed where they were. If I didn't get the job, I couldn't stay where I was. I was sure that after eighteen months of watching me teach and interacting with me as a faculty member, the search committee knew everything they needed to know. The less I said on interview day, the less chance I had of screwing things up. My goal was to survive the day and let my track record speak for itself.

One of them asked what it was like to be a female in the seminary community. I first answered how it had felt as a student: lonely. I told them that it could be lonely as a faculty member too. My voice cracked, and the table of men awkwardly waited for someone to say the right thing. Someone must have, though I don't remember who or what. When the dean finally—and mercifully—declared lunch over, I fled to my office to pull myself together before a final interview with the full faculty.

I was exhausted in every possible way, so I was especially grateful for faculty friends who came to the interview prepared with softball questions. Others had told me in advance what they were going to ask. The dean had several questions of his own, as did the search committee, but my friends carried the day . . . and me.

My last responsibility that day was teaching my Hebrew professor's class on the book of Jeremiah. I willed myself not to watch him jot notes as I taught, focusing instead on my carefully prepared lecture and elaborate PowerPoint presentation. I knew the material well, and I knew how to teach. I just had to outlast my nerves and my professor's poker face. When class ended, I bolted to my office for my coat. The dean caught up with me and said the day went very well. I thanked him and then nearly ran for my car.

Two candidates—and two more weeks—remained before the search committee would make their decision.

I waited.

Then I kept waiting.

My phone rang on a Monday morning. It was Alicia, the dean's administrative assistant. The dean wanted to meet with me that afternoon. I went expecting the worst but not really believing it would happen. The dean started by rehashing the search process— at least what the process had become. He finally got to the point: the seminary was hiring two candidates and I "came in third." He paused. I said nothing—but my heart pounded and my brain raced.

Then, knowing I had no backup plan, he offered me a part-time, one-year contract, split between the college and the seminary. I could stay in my office at the seminary. He gave me two weeks to think about it. I felt like a jilted girl who'd been asked to stay friends.

The faculty was upset—confused and disgusted, even. They were told that the university president would field their questions at the next faculty meeting—but he didn't, ever. Students were angry. They liked the candidates chosen just fine, but it made no sense to them that I wasn't hired.

It made no sense to most people, including the New Testament professor and dissenting vote on the search committee. We met for coffee several times, talked often on the phone, and emailed for weeks after the decision had been made. He was disturbed when he heard what the dean had told me before I came—namely, that one of the positions was all but mine and they would do a national search to fill the other. The committee understood from day one that both positions were to be filled by search and that I would be part of the search.

He also assured me that I didn't "come in third." It was a three-way tie—my evaluations were as high as those of the men who were hired. The only difference was that the retiring Old Testament professors wanted the other two candidates. He was outvoted, and his multiple attempts to change the outcome made no difference.

My brother-in-law, himself the victim of an employer's foul play, assured me that there was more going on than I could see: "Just remember, Wendy, it's not personal—it's always political. Always, always, always." I am sure that there were institutional politics in play, and maybe the dean was caught in them. But none of that excuses the injustice that was done.

The New Testament professor, a dear friend ever after, concluded, "Outrageously egregious events can only be explained as providential. Somehow God was in it because otherwise the outcome was bitterly ironic at best and unjustly random at worst."

God may have been in it, but I didn't like it.

And I still needed a job. The only option on the table was the dean's one-year, part-time offer.

THE WILDERNESS

I had two weeks to tell the dean whether I'd take the job or not. He was offering me a position that didn't exist at the time, and I suspect he cobbled together enough funds to create it because he felt bad about how things had gone. He also knew I didn't have a Plan B.

The last place I wanted to be was West Michigan. I asked my friends to pray, and they also offered advice—most telling me I should take the job, distasteful as the whole business was. It would buy me some time and give me a paycheck, such as it was, while I looked for the next thing. And it was only for a year.

They spoke wisdom. I accepted the contract, with the caveat that if I found another job I could leave.

About a week later, I received an email from someone at a digital media company that produced resources for the church. I recognized the sender's name because he had called me six months earlier about doing some freelance writing. Two of my colleagues from the Hebrew program in Madison worked at the same company on the West Coast, and both had given him my name when he was looking for writers. At the time, I was embroiled in part-time teaching and full-time candidating, and I'd told him I wasn't interested.

This time, not knowing what had just happened at the seminary, he wanted to know my employment status and if I was interested in talking about a full-time job. He was assembling a team of biblical scholars to write resources for laypeople.

It was a gift straight from God—a full-time job that seemed to fit my gifts and passions, at least some of them, and a ticket out of town.

But the West Coast was far away from everything and everyone I'd ever known. And the position represented a paradigm shift in what I thought God wanted me to do, what I'd just spent twelve years and thousands upon thousands of dollars preparing to do. Rather than teaching full-time and writing on the side, I'd be doing the opposite.

I spent Easter with my uncle and aunt, and we googled everything we could about the company and the boss. My uncle observed that the boss didn't lack for confidence, but he was also young and relatively accomplished—things that often go together. We talked through the pros and cons of accepting the position or staying where I was. I thought long and hard about moving across the country by myself.

What it finally came down to is that the job looked perfect on paper—metaphorically speaking, since nearly everything the company did was digital—and it could not have come at a better time. God had pulled another surprise on me.

With my mind mostly made up, I flew out for a visit. When I talked with the boss and the leader of my team, they told me how they saw me fitting in and what I would bring to the team that nobody else did. It mattered to them that I'd taught fifth grade and so had the ability to format information in an understandable way. They liked that I had experience writing full-length books for laypeople and that I'd also successfully completed a dissertation. They considered my freelance editing and the time I'd worked in a publishing house valuable. Everything on my résumé seemed to be meaningful, and the job they laid before me required a convergence of my varied experiences. I felt that God was making some sense of my meandering career path. For the first time in a long time, I felt appreciated and valued for exactly who I was and where I'd been.

The wife of one of my Madison friends drove me around town looking at apartments, and I found a two-bedroom condo with plenty of windows. I had a delightful dinner with a group of women from the department. On my last day I drove my rental car around the area to take in some West Coast beauty.

I flew back home and booked a mover (with a higher price tag and better reputation than the last one). I notified the dean via email that I wouldn't be fulfilling my contract, and then I recruited Suzy to travel across the country with me and help me get settled. I was nervous—scared, really—but also excited. There would be a lot to learn and an enormous amount of change, but I was ready for a fresh start. If the job didn't turn out to be a good fit, at least I'd be drawing a full-time paycheck while I looked for the next thing.

On a Thursday afternoon in mid-August, the moving van pulled away from my Michigan apartment and started its journey west. I stayed the night with friends before driving to Wisconsin for the weekend. On Monday morning, I picked up Suzy at dawn's early light for our week-long trek across the country.

We raced across Wisconsin, Minnesota, and South Dakota to Wall Drug on day one. On day two we pushed ahead to the outskirts of Yellowstone. After a day of sightseeing, we drove to within five hours of our final destination, and when I finally parked in front of my new apartment on Friday afternoon, we both could've kissed the ground. A "Welcome Home" balloon bobbed outside my front door, alongside a plant, a grocery bag of goodies, and a coffee maker on loan—a gift from one of the women at work. When Suzy and I found the condo complex's mailboxes later in the day, I discovered a handful of cards from faraway friends. I felt missed and welcomed all at once.

The Pacific Northwest was unusually sunny for the time of year, and the good weather made for a cheery welcome. While we waited several days for the mover to arrive, Suzy and I explored my new town and took care of errands. We stocked the refrigerator, got my new driver's license and license plates, and found the insurance agent. After the mover came, Suzy stayed several more days to help set up my apartment—every box unpacked and put away, every picture hung. I dropped her off at the airport on Labor Day weekend and returned to my new home with only a handful of loose ends left to tie.

My first week of work passed in a blur of newness. After a day of orientation meetings, I settled into my work space. My team shared an open area, a sort of bullpen separated from similar areas on our floor by a four-foot-high wall. Two rows of tables, our workstations, lined the walls and faced each other, a center aisle between them. A pair of computer monitors on each table shielded us from looking directly at coworkers across the aisle, and I positioned a bookcase next to my chair for a bit more privacy.

It seemed less than ideal for productivity, but white noise from the heating/cooling system muffled most voices. None of our computers had external speakers; everyone wore headphones. Aside from a handful of occasional annoyances, I didn't mind having colleagues in such close quarters. My office at the seminary had been a haven, but it had also been isolating; most professors had either worked from home or kept their doors closed.

The company culture was casual and generous. Plenty of employees, though few in my department, wore T-shirts, shorts, and flip-flops to work. The main break "room" took an entire floor, complete with couches, table tennis, a pool table, and video games. Complimentary pop, an array of other beverages, and all the espresso you could drink were in ready supply. Those of us who didn't work directly with customers could set our own hours.

But the casual environment did not extend to performance expectations. The tech industry moves quickly, and people who didn't keep up or measure up were fired. It happened regularly. At the end of my third week, one of my teammates disappeared. Department chatter said the boss told him he wasn't cut out for the fast-paced environment. I hoped I was.

The pace of production and its accompanying expectations concerned me, but I was also apprehensive about making the transition to a for-profit business. Most of my work experience was in the nonprofit sector—education and church ministry, where the bottom line had mattered a great deal in terms of keeping the doors open, but it didn't really matter at my desk. All I had to do was my part to make the classroom or the congregation the best it could be. Now I was in a company where the bottom line seemed to be everybody's business. Making money was the order of every day.

My actual job was, by design, a work in progress. The company mentality was to hire qualified people, discover how they could best contribute, and then craft jobs that positioned them to grow. The sky was the limit. Employees were encouraged to try new ideas if they could benefit the company. When people succeeded, they could more or less write their own job descriptions. I was surrounded by people who had done just that—departments that existed because an employee had an idea and ran with it.

My boss was one of these people. After only a few years at the company, he was head of a department he'd had the vision and the chutzpah to create. When I had interviewed with him in the spring, I'd found him likable. He was a go-getter, but the world needs go-getters.

The first project I worked on was a series of small group studies on Bible characters. Each book required digging into the biblical text and background and then crafting a meaningful study for nonbiblical scholars. The series was a big part of the boss's pitch to me before I took the job, and it had captured my interest because it involved careful work with the biblical text and creativity. Maybe I should have asked, but I assumed the series was typical of the work the boss was hiring me to do: write about the Bible in creative and meaningful ways for people in the pew.

After I sorted out what to do and how to do it, I tried to figure out how to do it faster—a department priority, I quickly learned. I also did some editing of earlier components in the project. My team leader was thrilled with my edits and talked to the boss about having me do more—taking some off his plate. The boss was reluctant, wanting me to focus on writing first, but my team leader talked him into it.

When I finished edits on the first chapter, which took a full day of work, I thought it was better. More importantly, I thought it represented what they wanted. The boss cranked up the heat on the project, and when I told my team leader I didn't know if I could finish the rest in time, he talked with the boss. Then I was summoned to meet with the boss.

He started by saying he had looked at my edits and thought I had made things worse. The time I spent was wasted, and now someone had to spend time fixing what I did—tripling the initial cost. He walked me through a paragraph or two and told me what it should look like, what he would change, and so on. Then he said, "If we had contracted this work to you, you'd be slashed. But as an employee . . ."

Well, I suppose that was good news.

I didn't think he was being entirely fair, but I didn't argue with him. It wasn't worth it. Instead, I told him what I understood the expectations to be and, given what he had just said, that I didn't feel like my role had been clearly communicated. He wasn't mad, but his brashness reduced me to tears. He sent me home with a book on writing. One of my sympathetic coworkers told me she read the book every year or two. It was the way we needed to write for the company.

Determined to do better, I read the book that weekend and reframed the way I thought about my work writing. The boss (and company) didn't want *my* voice; they wanted the *company* voice.

122

That was fair. They issued the paychecks, so I would learn to write that way.

My team leader apologized for what had happened. He had worked for the boss for more than a year and had learned how to do it well. In fact, he was one of several people I had talked with before accepting the position, and he had told me then, as everyone did, that the boss was great. He just took some getting used to.

But I struggled to see what was "great" about him. He was obsessed with making money. Admittedly, bosses need to be, to some extent at least, but not every boss carries it like a clipboard. Our weekly department meetings revolved around how to increase our profits—basically, work faster. He gave us lessons in project management. He lectured us on how to stay focused and organize our days to accomplish more. He admonished us to always think about the cost of doing things—such as helping a colleague with something if it wasn't our job. He told us repeatedly to look for ways to make ourselves more valuable to the company (and so also get raises). He preached to us about production management and business development from the book of Proverbs. He counseled us to use his principles in our personal lives too—you know, to get more done.

Maybe my younger colleagues weren't put off by his condescension. Maybe they found his advice helpful. But nearly twenty years his senior, I could barely stand to listen to him.

Worse than annoying, though, his management style was demoralizing. A month after I started, he implemented a project management system that used detailed statistical analysis to increase productivity. The boss set daily word count goals for us to hit—starting with two thousand words a day, what he considered a soft pitch ("I can hit two thousand words by 10:00 a.m."). We submitted our daily counts in weekly reports, and in return, he distributed graphs of the team's weekly average, our individual performances, and the incremental increases he expected for the next week. Some of my teammates pushed back, encouraging the boss to think in terms of a project's scope rather than its exact word count—but the boss was set on numbers. He liked to remind us that he wasn't asking us to do anything he hadn't done himself.

I rarely hit his two-thousand-words-a-day goal, but he offered his encouragement one week when I reached nearly seventeen hundred words: "You should hit two thousand words in the next week! As you know, that's what we expect from our writers."

As if I could forget.

Department veterans told me that things hadn't always been so bad. I had the misfortune of starting when the company was tightening its belt and making a big push for year-end income. This push trickled down to my boss, who felt the pressure—and responsibility—to make our department succeed and keep us employed. I could appreciate that. What I could not appreciate, however, was his inability to lead a department that consisted of more than its projects. He once said that every time we got up to get coffee, he saw dollar signs on the back of our heads—though he quickly assured us that, of course, he didn't think we shouldn't take coffee breaks. When it came to communicating value and affirmation to his team, he had the interpersonal skills of a porcupine.

To escape the insanity, I started taking advantage of the company's flexibility with respect to time and place of work. I adjusted my hours, starting before 6:00 a.m., taking a short lunch or eating at my desk, and leaving by 2:30 most days. On Wednesdays I worked from home. I tried to keep my head down and do my job, attracting as little attention as possible so as to minimize contact with the boss.

What I couldn't escape was the monotony. I had been told the job would have a variety of projects. New ideas made for a steady supply of possibilities. But possibilities were not realities. Where the rubber met the road—or where our fingers met the keyboard—there was only one project: the one that was making the most money. This meant that, not long after I started, the project I'd been working on got shelved. The series wasn't profitable enough. I was assigned to a different project, which had no room for creativity but at least involved plenty of time in the biblical text. Then about six months later, I was pulled from that project to work on another that took me out of the text altogether.

I languished in the tedium for months, my word counts nowhere near the boss's projections. I had told him that I functioned best with a variety of tasks, but he did not hear me. Coworkers fortunate enough to be working on multiple assignments passed off some of their smaller projects when they could, and I loved them for it.

In the middle of this boredom, the boss instituted monthly one-on-one "catch-up" meetings to improve communication. We each met individually with his assistant to talk about how things were going, what we'd like to work on, and anything else we wanted the boss to know. In my meetings, I expressed frustration and discouragement at the lack of variety in my assignments. But nothing changed.

Then the boss implemented weekly "tune-in" meetings with him every Tuesday morning. Each of us was to meet alone with him for five minutes, in which we would ask questions and express concerns. We were to be in charge of the meeting. In my first "tune-in," I expressed a desire for the department and company to better support the individual scholarship of their PhDs—people they'd hired because of their degrees. The boss reminded me that the company needed to be profitable, then he assured me he understood the challenges of being an academic and working full-time. That afternoon, we received notification of a required training session on being an academic in the department and the company, including the boss's thoughts on how we could accomplish more in less time.

I brought coffee cake for my colleagues as penance. And I spent the rest of the week trying to think of something for my next "tune-in" that wouldn't trigger another lecture. One of my coworkers gave me an idea that came out of a conversation he'd had with the boss where he had learned the boss's idea of leadership: first, the boss believed he had to be exponentially better at doing our jobs than we were, and second, he considered it his responsibility to coach us in our jobs. This was bizarre to me, so I decided to ask him about it.

Mostly, my plan was to get him talking about himself so I wouldn't have to say much.

I should have found a different topic. My five minutes turned into thirty, and before he was done, the boss informed me that I was the unhappiest person on the team and that I was lowering team morale. He followed up with an email summary of our meeting, offering his advice on how to improve and suggesting that I think about whether his department and the company were really the best fit for me.

He hadn't fired me, but I could see his hand reaching for the wall, pen poised. Beyond that, these were egregious accusations and, if true, he should have fired me.

I reached out to a handful of coworkers I trusted. After I processed their feedback, I responded in writing to the boss: "As I considered your assessment of my attitude and the ways you perceive I have reflected it, I think one of the problems here is personality—namely, you and I are night-and-day different. You are an off-the-charts extrovert. I, well, I'm not. I hide behind my desk from extroverts. You and I have totally different approaches to people and relationships."

Then I provided a long list of ways I had demonstrated to my colleagues that I valued them and the team. Most of these things happened behind the scenes, as befits an introvert, and most of them the boss had no way of knowing about, which is why I told him.

I addressed possible reasons for his perception of me, since I knew it didn't come from my colleagues. I explained some of my behavior that he may have interpreted through his extrovert lens—and thus misinterpreted.

I also suspected that one source of his perception was my conversations with his assistant at our monthly "catch-up" meetings: "Have I expressed frustration and unhappiness at my meetings? Absolutely—growing frustration and increased unhappiness, in fact, as my needs and concerns seem to go unheard. My drumbeat concern since I interviewed more than a year ago has been the lack of variety. When alternate tasks have been sparingly passed to me, I have gobbled them up. . . . I have felt like no one with power to change anything has really cared that I've languished in single, multimonth projects."

I don't remember if the boss thanked me for responding and explaining. It didn't really matter. What mattered is that he didn't fire me.

Tiptoeing around conversations with him was emotionally grueling. Every Monday night I went to bed hoping I'd wake up with a migraine on Tuesday so I could call in sick.

I believe he meant well. He was doing what he believed his job to be, and he was doing it within the confines of his particular context. Everyone has their context. His was youthful ambition, boundless energy, and a degree of success that drove him toward more. By contrast, I was at midlife and coming out of an environment where I'd been professionally wooed and courted (with a refrigerator, even!) and then inexplicably dumped at the altar. I was still reeling from the injustice and disappointment of it all. I wasn't interested in professional "success," as the boss might have defined it. I longed for a place that wanted *me*, not just a cog in the wheel of production. I yearned for a job that provided safety and security, not the fear of failure and being fired. I had hoped that God's surprise turn of events would take me to a place of thriving.

It hadn't. And I was confused, all over again.

I covertly explored other possibilities in the company, in search of a better fit—a place where the boss wouldn't be breathing down my neck as he counted my words and where I might actually use the degree I had worked so hard to earn. If I were really fortunate, it would also be a job I loved—or at least enjoyed more than the one that looked much better on paper than it ever had in real life. A few coworkers gave me some ideas to pursue, but despite numerous conversations over coffee, I was unable to gain traction on any of them.

Eventually, I started looking for jobs outside the company. I had resisted doing so for months, convinced that God had brought me to this place, and I was going to give it my best shot. But in the dreariness and despair of my first Pacific Northwest winter, I could hardly stand the thought of spending too many more in similar circumstances. I started watching academic job postings again, and I added church positions to my search filters. Maybe I could be a pastor of women or educational ministries. Maybe I could be an associate pastor. Earlier in my life and even career, I would not have considered "pastor" to be a possibility for me as a woman. But the longer I lived in the biblical text and in the church, the fewer good reasons I found to oppose the idea. I may not have been *comfortable* with women serving in every church capacity, but I realized my discomfort was cultural and not theological.

I pinned a US map on my living room wall and used sticky flags to mark where I'd sent applications: Minnesota, California, South Carolina, North Carolina, Texas, Massachusetts, Arkansas, Kansas, Iowa, Illinois, Washington, Ohio. Really, I didn't care where in the Lower 48 I went.

One by one, the sticky flags came down. For reasons I could not fathom, God wanted me at the Edge of Nowhere doing a job I loathed under a boss who made the work even worse. I came across an Elisabeth Elliot quote and put it under the plexiglass on my desk: "The job has been given to me to do. Therefore it is a gift. Therefore it is a privilege. Therefore it is an offering I may make to God. Therefore it is to be done gladly, if it is done for Him. Therefore it is the route to sanctity. Here, not somewhere else, I may learn God's way. In this job, not in some other. God looks for faithfulness."[3] I read those words every day, all day.

Not only did I not love my job, I was having trouble finding anything in my new town to love. I liked my colleagues and the people I had met at the church I was attending, but rare were the occasions we did anything outside work or church. I tried, but most of my efforts ended with me doing something by myself or, more likely, just staying home alone. After a while I concluded, with no hard feelings, that I needed them more than they needed me.

I adopted a tabby cat that a coworker with a growing family and a small apartment needed to give up. I'd never cared much for cats, growing up in a house with a mom who loved dogs and wrinkled her nose at the thought of cats. But I was desperate, and even my mom conceded that I'd appreciate the company of a furry friend, even if it was a cat.

I was delighted when Calvin proved easy to love. But apparently, I wasn't as easy to love. Calvin missed his former life, which was significantly more interesting than mine, and after several weeks in my quiet apartment, he made his unhappiness known on my new carpet, which the landlord had installed when the previous resident and his cats had moved out. I troubleshot with my coworker and the vet, and Calvin finished a course of meds. But it became clear that Calvin and the carpet could not peacefully coexist. Calvin's family had said they would take him back if things didn't work out, so on a teary afternoon, I returned my little buddy to his real home and then went to Trader Joe's to buy myself flowers and frozen foods for the rest of the week. When I vacuumed later and found one of Calvin's mouse toys under the couch, I pinned it on the bulletin board next to my desk to remember him.

Shortly after I had adopted Calvin, I met Harry. Harry was my eighty-year-old neighbor. His apartment was a stairwell over from mine, so we had only ever seen each other in the parking lot. One afternoon when I pulled into my parking spot after work, he was standing next to his car three spaces over. "Hey!" he yelled when I got out of my car. "I want to meet you."

I learned that Harry was pretty much the neighborhood watch. On account of bad lungs, he was on oxygen and spent a lot of time in his easy chair watching out the window. He knew I left early for work every day and that I came home early. I told him I had just gotten a cat. He knew: "It's orange and sits in the window." He was a vast wealth of knowledge about happenings in the condo complex.

After that, we would wave and call out greetings in the parking lot. I actually considered inviting him, along with the couple whose

129

living room wall I shared, to dinner during the long bleak winter. But I never got around to actually doing it.

Then my pastor posted on Facebook that he had free tickets for a swing band concert near my apartment. He played saxophone in the band. I thought it sounded like fun and wanted to go. But my next thought was, *Who would I go with?* I started at the top of my very short list. As I was writing an email to the first person on the list, I remembered she was out of town. Strike one. I emailed the second and while I waited for a response, I realized it was Mother's Day weekend, and friend number two was a mother, who had also recently told me she was crazy busy for the next few weeks. Sure enough, strike two. My last shot was the coworker who'd left the "Welcome home!" balloon at my door when I arrived in town. She had another commitment that night. Strike three.

I mentally scrolled through my contact list for anyone I knew well enough to ask. Nobody seemed like the right fit. Then Harry flitted through my mind.

"Nah," I said aloud. "That's crazy."

My next thought was from a book I'd read that suggested sometimes paying attention to "crazy" thoughts and just doing them because often they are promptings from the Holy Spirit. I decided that if all the stars aligned—or if the Spirit moved in a really obvious way—I would ask Harry. Basically, I'd do it if we ran into each other in the parking lot that afternoon, and the whole thing didn't seem too weird.

When I got home from work, neither Harry nor his car was in the parking lot. I went jogging, and when I got back, his car was still gone. I puttered at a few things inside, checking out the window periodically for his car, and finally decided to take my shower. I dumped my sweaty clothes in the laundry basket and took one last peek out the window. Harry was just pulling in. The stars were going to have to align better than that; I was not going to hustle back into my sweaty clothes (or any clothes, for that matter) and dash downstairs to catch him.

After my shower, I ate dinner and regrouped for an evening at my desk. I turned on my computer, made a cup of tea, and glanced out the window. There was Harry, fussing around in his car, bent over the floor of the front seats. I watched for a couple minutes, no idea what he was doing. It was obvious he wasn't going anywhere fast, so after another mental round of *I can't ask Harry. I barely know him*, I decided to take my trash out to the dumpster and see what happened.

En route to the dumpster, I stopped at my car to grab a stash of junk mail to add to the trash. As I opened my car door, Harry called out, "I'm having the d*mnedest time! Could you help me?" God has an extraordinary sense of humor.

I walked over to see what the blankety-blank problem was. He had lost his cell phone in the car and couldn't find it. He held up a second phone and said he could hear the first phone ring when he called. He called the number for me, and I performed the gymnastics necessary to retrieve his phone from deep under the front seat.

We stood and talked for a while, and I thought, *Okay, God really couldn't make this any more obvious.*

"So, I have a crazy question for you." I told him I had a friend who was playing in a swing band concert on Saturday night, and I really wanted to go but couldn't find any friends to go with me, and—

He interrupted, "And you don't want to go alone?"

"Right," I said. "Do you want to go?"

He thought it sounded fun, and did I want to get dinner beforehand? Then he asked if I knew how long the concert would last. I didn't know but said I would ask my friend. He pointed to the meter on his portable oxygen tank and said, "I need to make sure I have enough oxygen in my tank." I'd never had a date tell me that before.

Harry gave me his number. He also said I should come over to visit him sometimes.

On Saturday evening, Harry and I met at his car in the parking lot—he with two oxygen tanks in his backpack and I with two tickets in my purse. After dinner at the nearby Applebee's (his treat) and a delightful concert at the community center, we returned to the condos. When we parted ways, I thanked my new friend for sharing the evening with me.

I quickly learned that Harry had never met a stranger. He didn't really need any more friends. But I did. I called him on occasion, and we talked when we met in the parking lot. I discovered he loved cars—he loved to drive them, buy and sell them, collect them. In the span of his eighty years, he had owned nearly two hundred cars. He told me he had sold a good one to buy an engagement ring for his first wife when he returned from Korea, and years later he had sold another one to buy a house for his second wife. In hindsight, he said he'd rather have had the cars.

In the spring, Harry's red Thunderbird convertible came out of winter storage. It was a sweet car and when I told him so, he asked if I'd like to go for a ride sometime. On Father's Day we cruised the Pacific Northwest countryside, top down. My hair was a disaster, but I couldn't wipe the smile off my face. We ended up at Sonic for hot dogs before calling it a very good day. Harry had a daughter about my age, but they had long been estranged. He may not have needed friends, but I think he needed a daughter.

For his June birthday, I made his favorite cake, but I don't think he ate any of it. He wasn't eating much of anything. The doctor called on his birthday with news that his persistent stomach trouble was cancer. At the urging of his longtime friends, Harry subjected himself to chemo and radiation that summer—a cure that nearly killed him. On Labor Day, his doctor (who seemed to have a knack for ruining special days) called to tell him that nothing had worked. And he had a spot on his liver.

Harry stopped driving in early September—a fate nearly worse than death for him—and when I noticed that he hadn't been out, I called to see if he wanted me to get his mail. The condo mailboxes were a couple blocks away, and on account of his bad lungs, Harry had always zipped over in his gray Scion, what he called "the box," to pick up his mail.

"Well, sweetheart, that would be very nice!"

Nearly every day until he was moved to hospice four months later, I delivered Harry's mail late in the afternoon and then spent a few minutes watching TV and visiting with him. His friends knew me as the "mail girl."

After Harry died, his caregivers knocked on my door with a gift from Harry—ten one-hundred-dollar bills tucked in a "thank you" card. Harry had been someone for me to love in my new town—and I realized I'd been someone for him to love too. I was going to miss my friend, who had cleared a few clouds out of my thick gray sky.

Three unexpected events also helped clear a few clouds around the same time. The first happened in December, when I was seated on a jury for two full weeks. I'd always considered a jury summons a bit of a hassle, but this time it felt like a Christmas miracle. I joyfully performed my civic duty in exchange for two weeks of government-mandated vacation from the boss's word-counting.

A second Christmas miracle happened just before the New Year, when I received a call from a search committee that had eliminated me from their pool of candidates for a teaching position months earlier. Their search hadn't ended well, and they'd started over. Would I be available for a Skype interview?

The third event stunned me. It was a glee-filled gift straight from heaven for the new year, and I received it in the boss's office, of all places. For several months I had been working on projects that were part of a new company venture. They were even more monotonous than earlier projects, but since they didn't involve word counts, I considered them a welcome reprieve. In January, a week before Harry died, bigger wigs than the boss decided the new venture needed to be a separate department. The boss called me to his office to tell me about the changes.

Then he said, "I know you don't like my leadership style, and this may be a better fit professionally for your skills." Was I interested in transferring to the new department, effective immediately? For reasons I can only attribute to the stoic self-possession I inherited from my Dutch-German father, I responded by requesting twenty-four hours to think about it. My Madison friend Loralee later asked me why I didn't grab the offer and run for my life.

I may have floated home from work that day. It didn't matter that I'd be doing the same mind-numbing job in the new department. What mattered is that I no longer answered to the boss. For the first time in nearly a year and a half, I felt free.

Now, to prepare for that interview. I had fresh hope of getting out of the Pacific Northwest altogether—and not be so miserable trying.

THE AVALANCHE

One holiday weekend, desperate for something to do, even if I had to do it alone, I took a day trip to a nearby island where I'd heard there was good hiking. My impression was that the main trail would take me to the highest point of the island and offer a to-die-for panoramic view of an archipelago to the west and the mainland to the east.

Once on the island, I stopped for a tourist map. The gal who gave it to me warned that the first fifteen minutes of the trail were steep. I found the trailhead, parked my car, and set out with my backpack. My plan was to get to the top of the island, eat a peanut butter and jelly sandwich, take in the spectacular view for a few minutes, and then head back to my car—mission accomplished.

After a steep climb that lasted more than fifteen minutes and then an endless trail that offered few flat stretches, I was pretty sure my information source had never actually been on the trail. Markers were almost nonexistent, the woods were dense and deserted, and the trail just kept going up.

Long past the point I thought I might die and be eaten by wild-life before anyone discovered me, I reached a designated overlook. Climbing between trees to get to it, I wondered if I had arrived at my destination. I snapped a few pictures of islands in the distance. The view was nice, but it wasn't what I was expecting. I returned to the trail and pressed on. Surely there was more ahead. The brush grew thick—the trail obviously less traveled—and I grumbled about the lack of signage. Ten sweaty minutes later, I'd had enough bush-whacking and turned around.

I was more than a little disappointed. What I had seen was beautiful (and, I later learned, was the destination)—it's not like I see an archipelago every day of the week. But I had expected more. I envisioned standing at the tippy top of the island, taking in a sweeping panoramic view. At the very least, there should have been a sign that said, "This is it! You've made it!" Instead, I was left confused, wondering if there was something more. Had I missed a path that would've taken me to something even better?

I had moved across the country to launch a new life, expecting that God had redirected my midlife path for an unexpected good. I anticipated a career that drew together my experiences and educa-tion in ways I could not have envisioned. I assumed I would find a new community of people to be a family where I had none.

None of these things had happened. I was confused, to say the least. I was also angry and hurt. Why had God moved me to what felt like the edge of nowhere for nothing? Hadn't he seen me through twelve years of graduate school in preparation for some-thing? Hadn't he closed—slammed even—doors that should, by all accounts, have led to a meaningful career? Why had he given me a full résumé of qualifications if I did not need them? Worse, why did he seem to tease me with jobs I couldn't have?

I didn't get the teaching job. In an all too familiar pattern, I was a finalist, one of two candidates invited to campus for a multiday interview. And again, I was not the one hired. Thankfully, the only drama associated with this disappointment was that I learned the news on Facebook before the school's dean had a chance to call me.

But I was devastated. Months earlier I'd accepted the disappointment of my candidacy sailing off into space. Why had God brought it back—only to have it burn up in reentry? Why couldn't he have left well enough alone?

Some friends tried to encourage me, saying, "There's another hiring cycle coming," as if I should expect that to go differently than the previous three cycles I'd been part of. Other well-meaning friends said God must have something better, but I wondered. No, I disagreed. This "bigger and better" theology—this idea that if God denies you something good, then he must have something better for you—falls apart when you read what the Bible really says and when you acknowledge what Christian experience throughout history affirms. One of my wisest friends said, "There are not words for this. We hold to a God who is good."

I gave up job hunting for Lent that year and grieved. I considered moving to Minnesota, where Loralee and her family were living by then. Maybe I could find a job there. Another friend from Madison days had done that successfully and recommended it. But given my success with "choose your own adventure" jobs, I thought better of it.

And I wrestled, not for the first time, with questions of vocation and calling. Over the years I had read and heard plenty on these matters, along with the idea of finding God's perfect fit for my abilities, experiences, and passions. I considered my vocational calling to teach and write about the Bible. These were the things God had prepared, impassioned, and equipped me to do. Surely he would make a way for me to serve him with everything he had given me.

But would he? Was this something that he had, in fact, said he would do?

About the same time, I was also reading some material on the book of Job. The author contended that the book is less a test of Job than it is a test of God's way of dealing with people. If God doesn't bless his followers with good things, will they still follow him? Will people follow him for nothing, or at least what looks like nothing?

I was certainly no Job, and I had plenty more than "nothing"—in this life and the life to come. But like Job, I felt the angst of confusion and even betrayal at the hands of God. What had I done to deserve a mind-numbing job in a lonely environment? Would I follow God for nothing? Would I follow him for his sake, not mine?

A friend who'd survived midlife told me that it's often a time of stripping away. Another friend said it was a time of letting go. I was finding it to be a combination of both—the dance of divine sovereignty and human responsibility. God had stripped away opportunity after opportunity. He had taken away the very things he'd set me up to do. He had removed me from places of familiarity and friendship. But I also needed to let go of dreams—dreams of a teaching job or any other meaningful job, for that matter. I needed to let go of my expectations for a fulfilling career. I had to release my grip on what I thought my life would look like. For reasons I did not understand, God wanted me where I was, doing what I was doing.

The long Lenten season ended and Easter came—as it does every year this side of the cross. The winter rains dried up, leaving behind a rainbow of crocuses, daffodils, and hyacinths across the Pacific Northwest.

As my surroundings burst into bloom, I realized that I was going to be okay. Nothing had changed about my circumstances. I still spent eight hours a day logging time at a job that I found dull as doorknobs. The handful of résumés I sent into cyberspace still returned only rejections. I had no better success finding friends and building community. The wilderness stretched as far as I could see. But for once in a very long time, I could see the wilderness with joy and not despair. God knew where I was and what I needed, and maybe what I needed most was to learn the way of discipleship—faithful obedience for no obvious return on the investment.

That summer I decided to start the process of buying a condo. Like the Israelites in Babylonian exile admonished by Jeremiah to build their houses and settle down, to plant their gardens and eat what they produced, it was time for me to embrace where I was, for however long God wanted me to be there. Maybe he would provide a way out, but in the absence of a prophetic word, it was impossible to know. Two years had passed already. Who was to say another five wouldn't go by before I'd realized it?

I thought about my holiday hike. I had been so focused on the destination and what I expected to find at the top of the island that I'd missed most of the journey itself. I'd missed the chance to step into a field of lush fern. I could have knelt to examine the moss that covered a log like a pile of Easter basket grass. I didn't stop to listen to the wind rustle the dense foliage. If I had bothered to enjoy where I was, I wouldn't have been so disappointed by where I ended up.

In July I met with a loan officer at the bank, and I made an appointment with a real estate agent. On the Friday I hoped to meet with the agent, I was invited to a small group lunch with an Old Testament professor who was in town teaching a class. I did not know the professor, but some googling informed me that he was in his late thirties. His online faculty bio said he'd sensed God's calling to teach the Bible, and especially the Old Testament, since his college days.

"Well, imagine that. And he got to do it. Yay, him," I muttered. Despite the progress I'd made accepting my circumstances, apparently I was not immune to sour grapes—or at least cynicism.

But because my thwarted calling wasn't the professor's fault and because someone else was paying for lunch, I went. Ed was an engaging guy, and I liked him immediately. He asked everyone around the table how we ended up in our present jobs. When he got to me, I answered matter-of-factly, "I'm here because, after several failed academic hiring cycles, I needed a job."

The topic then naturally turned to an Old Testament opening at his school. Having made up my mind to buy a condo, I had stopped looking at job postings and didn't know about the position. Ed was on the search committee, which had been trying for several years to hire someone. Each search had come up empty, for a variety of reasons, but Ed was obviously frustrated. It all sounded like a bit of a fiasco, so I jokingly said, "What you're saying is that I shouldn't apply?" Without missing a beat, he surprised me by replying, "No, I wish you would."

We talked a bit more about the school and the position. It was obvious that Ed loved the community and faculty there. He considered it a unique and special place. But he was also clear about my prospects: "You might get hurt. We might hurt you in this process." His years of search committee experience told him that.

I'd been hurt before—could it be any worse? I stewed about our conversation that afternoon and eventually canceled my appointment with the real estate agent. There was no sense looking for a condo unless I was sure I wasn't going to apply for a job several states away.

I wrestled all weekend with the decision. I knew a little about the school because the publishing house I had worked for during seminary had published some books by professors who taught there. I recognized that it was theologically conservative, as was I, but I wasn't sure *how* conservative—most specifically, what view they took on women in ministry. Obviously, they were open to a woman teaching men the Bible in a classroom setting, which is the extent of what I was interested in doing. But I needed to know whether they believed the Bible restricted women's ministry in the church and, more importantly, whether agreement with their position was a condition of hire. If so, I would not apply.

I scoured the school's website and waded through their doctrinal statement. It said nothing about the issue. They also had a second tier of beliefs, their theological distinctives, which included several items that a born-and-bred Baptist could affirm. Again, nothing about women and the church. I could tell that historically the school had held a moderately restrictive view and that many of its professors still did, but nothing on the website specifically addressed the issue. When I browsed the faculty pages, I stumbled across a name I recognized from my bookshelves: I owned her book on the equality of men and women in the church. That seemed as strong an indication as any that difference of opinion was okay.

By Sunday night, I had put the house hunt on hold. I would try for a teaching job one more time.

During the next week I updated my résumé, wrote a letter of interest, and put together a video of me teaching—the materials requested for application. A month later, I received a warm email from the search committee member tasked with candidate communication. He notified me that they had narrowed the field from more than fifty applicants to six, including me. Would I send some writing samples and a collection of student evaluations from classes I'd taught? He hoped these requests wouldn't "be overly burdensome in the midst of a busy fall," and he told me what the next steps in the process were and when I might expect to hear from him again. He ended by thanking me for my patience in an intense search process.

A week later, another cheery email came, beginning with the exclamation, "What a gift from God that we have so many qualified potential faculty members interested in joining our team!" The committee had met and narrowed the field to five, including me. Congratulations! The next step was a thirty-minute video call with the entire committee, in which the focus would be my approach to teaching Hebrew.

A successful Skype interview two weeks later moved me to the next stage of the process—a phone interview with one of the deans. In a friendly conversation that lasted nearly two hours, the dean walked me through the hiring process and told me what to expect along the way. Then he asked me what had happened with my advisor and original dissertation at UW–Madison and why I didn't get hired at the seminary in Michigan. I told him the honest truth as I knew it and gave him phone numbers of faculty who could answer additional questions. He was stunned by the story and expressed how sorry he was about what had happened to me.

For not the first time, I was surprised—and impressed—by the way the school was conducting its search. I can't speak for the hiring process in other fields, but in the academy, applicants are treated like faceless names at the top of a résumé. Even if you make it through multiple phases, you are a *candidate* more than you are a *person*. But this school treated me like a person—a friend, even. They kept me informed at each step, and everyone I interacted with was warm and affirming. Obviously, they cared about my ability to do the job, but it was clear that they cared more about me as a person. They were looking for someone who would fit into their community of trust and support.

In October I was invited to submit a nineteen-page application that included my personal testimony, educational theory, and detailed interaction with the school's doctrinal statement. I was told that the school was looking for professors who shared the convictions expressed in the statement, so if anything raised an issue for me, I should be sure to let them know. A couple weeks later, I received an email asking for clarification on my views on how the Bible records history, what I think of hell as a real place, and how God created humankind.

In November I attended the annual conference for biblical scholars, where I enjoyed a ninety-minute meeting with the search committee over coffee. And I did enjoy it—I felt as if I was becoming one of them. After the conference, I emailed to ask what the environment was like for women teaching the Bible. Two email responses from committee members and a phone call from the woman on the committee allayed any fears I had about the school being a safe and welcoming place for me to be.

Before Christmas I had another phone interview, this time with the chair of the Old Testament department. He was on his way to the airport, and we chatted informally for thirty minutes. When we finished, he said he would mark my application "ready for interview"—by which he meant a campus visit—but I still almost laughed out loud. I'd already had at least four interviews in as many months. The next day he emailed to thank me for taking time out of my busy day to talk with him. He said he was praying for me and the school in the process. He also wanted me to know that things would be quiet for a few weeks, but they'd be back in touch come January.

Sure enough, in early January I received an invitation to interview on campus. I boarded a plane at 5:00 a.m. on the appointed day in early February and arrived on campus in time for lunch with Dr. Eastwood, the seminary dean, for our first interaction. This was followed by a "doctrinal review" meeting with the Old Testament department chairman, whom I'd spoken with in December. Then I was ushered to the office of the university provost. The first day concluded with my teaching a Hebrew grammar class. Afterward, one of the committee members said I had hit a home run.

On the second day, I was allowed to sleep in before having lunch with the dean I'd spoken with at length earlier in the fall. That afternoon I taught a second class, specifically concerned with the world of the Old Testament. I tackled a difficult topic, surprising a couple committee members with my choice—but as I told them, I decided to "go big or go home." They both raved about how the class went, and another committee member called my lecture inspiring. The day ended with a lovely and relaxing dinner with the committee, and on Friday I flew home, overwhelmed with how good it all felt—a rare feeling after a campus visit.

A month later I was invited back for a second campus visit, the last stage in the arduous hiring process. I was told to expect a less stressful trip since I wouldn't be teaching any classes and had already met with nearly everyone involved in hiring. I was scheduled for leisurely meals with several seminary administrators, brief meetings with the university's vice provost and the president, an intense interview with more than a dozen department chairs, and a celebratory dinner with the search committee. With these events spread over three days, I planned to look for an apartment; one of the committee members had told me he and his wife found their house on his second campus visit.

My plane landed after dark, and I drove a rental car to the hotel. After my lunchtime responsibilities the next day, a friend in the area took me apartment hunting. That evening the seminary dean and his wife picked me up for dinner. Halfway through dinner, Dr. Eastwood asked my view on 1 Timothy 2. I stared blankly at him. Interviewers rarely asked me about New Testament texts, and never in any of my four hiring cycles had anyone asked about 1 Timothy 2—Paul's prohibition against women teaching or assuming authority over men. The dean's background was New Testament studies with a specialty in Paul's letters, so I assumed he was just exploring his own area of interest.

I hadn't looked at 1 Timothy in years. I knew it as the linchpin text in arguments for restricting women in ministry, but I didn't waste postage applying for jobs at schools that believed the restriction included the classroom setting. During my Madison tenure, I had worked through the issue of women in ministry, studying the primary texts and reading a handful of books—enough to reach a conclusion my conscience could live with before God. Then I put the books back on my shelf and returned to my Old Testament business.

I'm terrible at remembering the details of an argument, but I told the dean my conclusion about the passage. I recognized that it probably differed from his but thought nothing of it. I had been interacting with this school for eight months, and I knew there to be differing opinions on the issue among the faculty and administration.

Dr. Eastwood pushed back, pressing for particulars about Paul's use of Genesis 2 and 3. I had no better answers than my general conclusions but began wondering why he kept at it. Finally he said, "The reason I'm asking is because the department chairs will ask about this in your interview tomorrow morning."

I was surprised but thanked him: "Honestly, it's been several years since I worked through this issue. I don't remember every point of the debate. But now that I know it will come up tomorrow, I will go back to my hotel room and call a good friend, a New Testament professor, who shares my view. I will ask him the details of the position so I am prepared. Thank you for letting me know."

Our conversation moved to other matters, but the knot in my stomach ruined the rest of my dinner. I had expected to be grilled in my interview the next day, but about this? In all my interactions with this school, I'd never been asked about the issue of women in ministry, and it was the last thing I wanted to talk about in *any* setting, much less a job interview.

On the ride back to the hotel, I maintained amicable chatter with Dr. Eastwood and his wife in the front seat, but my attention was on a text conversation in my lap with my New Testament professor friend. "Are you home and available to talk?" He was. "I'm calling soon to talk about 1 Timothy 2."

Back in my hotel room, I called him. While he also was surprised at the turn of conversation, he was certain that the school simply wanted to be sure I had a reasoned position and that I wasn't pursuing some militant feminist agenda. They were more interested in *how* I approached the issue, which so often divides people, than *what* I had concluded—after all, it wasn't in their doctrinal statement or theological distinctives, so it couldn't be a condition of hire. His perspective as a senior scholar—and his bullet points for talking through 1 Timothy 2—helped me breathe a bit easier and get some sleep.

At 7:30 the next morning I met with the group of department chairs, which the seminary jokingly called the Sanhedrin. We talked for more than an hour, and I felt welcomed, affirmed, and comfortable with them. The question of women in ministry came up several times in a variety of ways, and I answered honestly, navigating the argument as best I could but also acknowledging that I hadn't spent much time in recent years dealing with the primary texts.

They finally called an end to the interview and dismissed me. In the hallway, I breathed a sigh of relief. I felt like I'd just finished a marathon—utterly exhausted but completely exhilarated at the achievement. I'd been a candidate since the first week of August; it was now mid-March, and I had survived. The next morning, I would meet with the university president and be offered a contract. Seeing this dream, this calling, fulfilled had been a long, painful journey, but I could see God's hand in the circuitous path I'd traveled.

I met my apartment-hunting friend at the front door of the seminary, free to think about where I'd be living in just a few short months. I was already planning the road trip Suzy and I would make that summer.

Several hours later, my friend dropped me off at the hotel. I had a few hours to relax before a celebratory dinner with the search committee. I kicked off my shoes and collapsed on the bed when I saw I had a voicemail. It was from Lori, the woman on the search committee and someone I considered a friend by this time. Warm and welcoming, Lori epitomized every encounter I'd had with the school.

"Wendy, this is Lori. Can you call me back when you have a chance? I wasn't able to be at the interview this morning, and I want to hear your perspective on what happened."

My heart started to pound. What happened? I'd had an intense but friendly interview and then looked for a place to live.

I pressed the ten digits of Lori's number into my phone and paced the hotel room floor. She answered and quickly got to the point: there was concern among the Sanhedrin about my view on women. Could I tell her what I had said so she could try to make sense of things? As she talked, I watched myself in the bathroom mirror. I knew where this was going and mouthed it to my reflection: "You are going to lose this job over *this* issue."

Eight months into the most rigorous interview process I'd ever been through, I'd been blindsided. I was baffled. What on earth had happened?

Lori said she wasn't sure where things stood with my candidacy, but the search committee still wanted to have dinner with me. We met later that evening, and they were nearly as upset as I was—another bafflement to me. Ed did his best to explain what had happened. The university did not have an official position on the role of women in ministry—which is why none of the documents I'd interacted with included it. It was not a condition of hire, and thus, apparently, the search committee was not allowed to ask about it. However, the seminary, a school within the university, had its own historic position on the issue and, for reasons I did not understand, *was* allowed to factor a candidate's view into their decision-making—yet, mysteriously, nobody had asked my view until twenty-four hours earlier.

In multiple conversations and interviews, I had been asked if I knew the historic position of the seminary on the role of women in ministry and if I was okay with it. I always responded honestly, "Yes, I know and respect the position. I have no problem working in an environment where that is the predominant position." It was, after all, where I had spent most of my life. I had no axe to grind for women's rights, and I had no intention of speaking directly to the issue in the classroom; my field was Old Testament studies, and the controversial texts about women in ministry are all in the New Testament. I did my best to avoid the topic altogether—personally and professionally—and I'd been pretty successful at it.

The search committee thought I should be hired. The seminary administration thought my view was incompatible with their view. The university held no such position on the matter.

When we parted ways after dinner, the committee told me the administration hadn't decided yet what to do about me. As soon as they had more information, they would let me know.

Still stunned—shell-shocked, really—I returned to my hotel room where I chatted online with Loralee and Kyle in Minnesota and then talked on the phone with my New Testament friend while I waited. The call came before I went to bed. The administration had decided to suspend my candidacy and allow me time to revisit the issue, since I had said repeatedly that I hadn't thought much about it for several years. The following morning, where my schedule had a meeting with the university president, I would meet with Dr. Eastwood instead.

Troubled sleep finally gave way to morning, but I awoke with a sick, sad feeling. I drank some coffee and nibbled at breakfast, packed my bags for travel, and drove to the seminary. Dr. Eastwood apologized for what had happened, that they had not discovered this issue much earlier in the process. Then he told me that the seminary's position functioned as a "third tier" of beliefs below the doctrinal statement and the theological distinctives. I had never seen it, and I told him so. He apologized again and told me it was in the seminary catalog, which I later found online. Tucked away on page 193 was a brief section titled "Women at the Seminary." Three short paragraphs spoke of "the equality of women and men" and "the giftedness and roles of women within the guidelines of Scripture concerning order and complementarity" and so on. I recognized the code language for the view that restricts women from at least some ministries in the local church, but the catalog hardly presented this as a belief required of everyone involved in the school. Nor had anyone ever brought it to my attention and said, "If this isn't you, you shouldn't apply for a job here."

The sticking point was my belief that the Bible does not restrict women from senior leadership in the church. I was clear when I spoke with the committee that I was not always *culturally* comfortable with this position, but theologically I did not have a problem with it. I was also clear that I had no aspirations for such leadership; I simply wanted to teach the Old Testament in a school setting. I also told them that I had no intentions of promoting my view and undermining the historic (and, as I'd just learned, actual) position of the seminary.

Dr. Eastwood expressed how much the entire seminary faculty and administration liked me. He said what an outstanding teacher I was and what good I could bring to their community. All these things were enough to make them hit "pause" instead of "stop" on my candidacy. He proposed that we all back away and take a breath. He asked, given my acknowledgment that I didn't remember the details of how I reached my conclusion, if I'd be willing to revisit the relevant texts over the next few weeks.

I really liked these people and their school. Despite the rigor of their process, they had been the easiest and most pleasant to work with of any school I'd interviewed with. From the beginning, they had treated me like a person and, as time went on, like a friend. Sure, they had bungled this—but they admitted it and apologized for it. They appeared to be a supportive, collegial community. It was a place I still wanted to be part of. I agreed to look through a book Dr. Eastwood gave me, written by one of their emeritus professors, as I went through the issue for myself again.

I flew home that afternoon, emotionally drained and profoundly discouraged. A week that had begun with such anticipation and excitement had turned into a nightmare. Instead of getting out of my dead-end job, I seemed more stuck than ever. Instead of being welcomed into a faculty family, I had been left out in the cold for reasons that made no sense.

As I plodded through my little project over the next few weeks, Lori called to check on me and to affirm that the search committee stood behind me. I appreciated her kindness. Faraway friends emailed and phoned to tell me they were praying for me. I trudged to work every day but laid lower than usual, unable to muster the emotional energy to interact with anyone who didn't already know what was going on.

On Good Friday I emailed a letter to the search committee—the results of my do-over study on the role of women in ministry. The bottom line was that I considered both our views defensible, but I still found mine more persuasive. I detailed my reasons but spent most of my letter on what I believed to be the most important issue in the question of men and women in ministry: what is best for a given church in its particular context. I concluded my letter by saying I'd be honored to partner with the faculty, "teaching men and women how to study the Bible and 'do ministry'—while in an environment where professors doggedly committed to community have different opinions on an issue that too often polarizes the church. What a marvelous way for students to learn how to be the body. If you invite me to be part of your community, I promise that I will carefully guard against this ever becoming a divisive issue, and I will welcome an environment of mutual accountability to make sure that never happens."

The school had just started spring break, so my email sat idle for a week. Before I'd heard any official response, Lori called again. She'd read my letter and wondered if I'd be willing to talk to another female professor at the university who was writing a book about the issue. She started to tell me about it, and I stopped her. "Lori, I appreciate what you are trying to do. But I am not going to discuss this any further if I need to arrive at a predetermined view to be hired. I cannot talk about this anymore. I am done."

And I was. The letter from Dr. Eastwood came a few days later. I was at work when it showed up in my inbox. He expressed his regret for how things had gone and did his diplomatic best to justify the school's decision. I forwarded his email to two colleagues at work—men I had worked with under the boss when I started at the company. They dropped everything to meet me for coffee. The first handed me his coffee card and said, "I have some free drinks on there. Go get something." The second shook his head at me and held out his arms, offering a hug. I took it—and to the extent I could in a public place without totally going to pieces, I sobbed.

The three of us sat in the coffee shop for a long time. I mostly cried, saying, "I cannot believe *this* is what it came down to." My friends grieved with and for me—and for what we all considered a defeat for the church. One of them pointed out the irony of Dr. Eastwood's letter and the committee's decision: "If I had been the candidate, they never would have asked my view on this issue. It wouldn't have even come up. They only asked it because you are a woman." It was impossible to know for sure if he was right, but I suspected he was.

Several members of the search committee reached out to me. Two of them emailed to ask if they could talk with me. Ed sent a note that he was deeply grieved, sad that his school had "failed to hire a truly exceptional teacher" and sad about how the process and decision had affected me personally. He repeated that the search committee had no reservations about my candidacy; the final decision had been out of their hands. I realized that Lori's earlier call had been a last-ditch effort by the committee to save my candidacy. Perhaps if I had agreed to talk with her friend, it would have made a difference; the book her friend ultimately wrote went on to win a prestigious award and was praised for its contribution to the debate.

But I simply couldn't do it anymore. This hiring cycle had been the last straw. I had nothing left.

And God knew it. He had given me all I could take—or taken away what he'd seemingly given me, depending how you looked at it—and when I finally said "I give up," he was ready for his next move.

THE DEAD END

The weekend before I received Dr. Eastwood's email ending my candidacy, two thoughts occurred to me. The first came with the force of reality: the school was not going to hire me. The second resurfaced from the ash heap, having first appeared the previous spring before I came to terms with my dismal career situation and decided to "build a house" and "plant a garden" where I was. Frustrated with dead ends in every direction, I'd considered quitting my job to find a new one in Minnesota, where Loralee lived with her family.

This time, however, I wondered about the possibility of keeping my despised job and working remotely from Minnesota. I desperately wanted to get out of the Pacific Northwest where I felt trapped. Geographically, I was stuck in a small town that required fourteen hours of taxi-bus-plane travel just to visit my family. Professionally, I'd been unable to find a more rewarding job, and I'd hit the ceiling on what my bosses would pay for my position. Socially, I'd failed to find a community of friends that needed me as much as I needed them. I was in search of a change, a shake-up of my circumstances in the hopes that their resettlement would resolve some of my distress.

I knew that moving back across the country wouldn't fix a lot of things, but it would at least put me where I had the nucleus of a community. It would give me people to love and a family to be part of, and maybe, just maybe, other good things would grow out of meeting that basic need. I did hope that moving to the Midwest would improve my employment opportunities—the Twin Cities alone are home to several Christian colleges, seminaries, publishers, and other parachurch organizations. But even if it didn't, being near friends and a half-day's drive from my family in Wisconsin was enough to make it worth the gamble. When I told Loralee that I was reconsidering this Plan B, she wryly said it was probably at least Plan K by now.

Dr. Eastwood's email arrived on a Tuesday morning, and by the end of that week, a friend had helped me put together a proposal for my bosses. Several weeks of negotiating resulted in a contract I was willing to live with, and I started packing. Unable to afford a mover this time, I reserved a U-Haul that a saint of a friend offered to drive. From several states away, Loralee helped me hunt for an apartment. I narrowed possibilities online, and she went to see them. When she toured a place just two miles from her house and reported back that I could do worse but probably wouldn't do better, I signed a lease.

Six weeks later, the clouds of the Pacific Northwest were in the rearview mirror of my little Elantra as I shadowed the U-Haul back across the country. The miles ahead had their own challenges. Like Montana's big sky, uncertainty stretched in every direction, but of one thing I was sure: I had to move. After several years of running into barricades, I'd finally found an open road, and I raced to get on it before it disappeared. I had no idea where the road went, but it didn't matter. I knew I had to go there.

A couple of male colleagues from UW–Madison days lived in the Twin Cities and weeks earlier had responded to my request for help unloading on the afternoon I arrived. One recruited a trio of twenty-somethings from his church, and the entire group emptied the U-Haul by the time Suzy arrived from Wisconsin. As my get-it-done sister carved paths through the boxes and furniture, I wandered in a stupor of exhaustion, ready to collapse and wishing to wake up to a new day where everything had been made right. But Suzy had come to help—and I needed it—so I willed myself to stay on my feet for a couple more hours.

It was a warm July night, and the apartment had been closed up for several weeks. We opened the windows for fresh air but soon realized it wasn't very fresh; cigarette smoke hit my nostrils, and I unraveled. Heaving myself over a tower of boxes, I wailed at my purpose-driven sister hefting boxes: "Oh, what have I done!" All but ignoring my distress, she said, "You moved."

There was more than one reason I always asked Suzy to help me move.

Loralee's family was on vacation when I arrived in town, but she had left me a house key. After a night of hard sleep at her house, Suzy and I got busy. I took my U-Haul-driving friend to the airport and joined Suzy's whirlwind at the apartment. By day's end, we had positioned the furniture and sorted the boxes, a good number of which were also unpacked. By the end of the next day, she had stored away the boxes, all emptied, for my next move—a task she had mastered by this time. Early the next morning, she drove back home, and I took stock.

The apartment had as much square footage as the one I'd left, but with only one bedroom instead of two. I used a corner of the large living room for my office and lined my bedroom with bookshelves. The small galley kitchen had all the essential appliances—refrigerator, stove, microwave, and dishwasher—but since space was minimal, nothing was standard size. At five-feet, six-inches tall, I could stand on tiptoes and peer over the top of the refrigerator, and my largest baking pans barely fit in the oven. I called it my Lilliputian kitchen. Open counter space measured in inches, and I had to use the adjacent dining room for storage and even some food preparation. The kitchen's best feature was a window at its far end.

The living room opened to a screened porch, which had seemed a nice feature in the absence of a balcony. I soon realized it robbed the main room of light, and with a downstairs neighbor who went through packs of cigarettes on his own screened porch, I rarely opened the sliding doors.

But the complex was quiet—except for Bentley, the dog across the hall whose barking spells prompted more than one complaint to management. And a coffee shop a mile away was an easy escape.

Best of all, Loralee was close by. When the dark solitude of my apartment became too much, I packed up my work and moved to a bright spot at her dining room table. Some days I brought my laundry basket, saving quarters and the hassle of the shared apartment laundry room. Loralee often worked at her desk downstairs, and I worked upstairs; we'd break for tea and cookies and then for lunch. We hadn't had so much time together since we were students in Madison nearly a decade earlier, and the regular reunions were balm for my battered soul.

On other days, Loralee and the kids stopped by my apartment, bringing bright zinnias or fresh vegetables from their garden. My collection of children's books and stuffed animals occupied the older kids, and Loralee brought some toys to leave at my place to entertain the youngest. I planned special events with each of the kids—baking bread with one and taking another to a Lego exhibit and another to an apple orchard. We all piled in their minivan for an outing to a local sculpture garden, and many evenings I joined hands around their dinner table. Rather than navigating winter driving to Wisconsin for two holidays in the span of weeks, I spent Thanksgiving with Loralee's extended family nearby.

I dearly loved Loralee and her family, and their presence provided support I needed. But I had no illusions that they would save me from my desperate life circumstances. I still lived alone and needed to clock forty hours a week at a job that bored and frustrated me. It wasn't a sustainable situation for the long haul, but I tried to make the best of it—believing that I was in a better place than where I'd been and trusting that somehow God was in it.

I broke up long mornings by jogging a route to the library and back, and in the afternoon I often went walking. The apartment complex was nestled in an established suburban neighborhood and was three blocks from a country club that sprawled on either side of the main street. Midcentury lots, with lush foliage and no two houses alike, ran along the thick tree line that surrounded the golf course and made soothing scenery.

Walking has always been one of the best ways to clear my head, sort out my life, and—on a good day—even make some sense of it. I had a lot of sorting out and making sense to do in the weeks and months after I moved to Minnesota.

We each grow up with landmarks and geographic boundaries that shape our life experiences. For me, my childhood home and neighborhood were bounded by the landmarks of the library, the ice cream shop, my elementary school, and our sledding destination, Killer Hill. As I grew older, I came to understand the importance of Lake Michigan in my mental topography. While we lived several suburbs away from the lake, it was nonetheless an integral part of life. Local weather reports regularly credited the lake for snow and icy winds in the winter ("lake-effect snow") and cool breezes that chilled in spring and relieved in summer ("cooler near the lake"). My sister and I spent our college summers filing invoices for a company within walking distance of the lakefront, and we often went that direction during our lunch hours. After college, I sometimes joined church friends for a trip downtown to rollerblade or walk the trails along the marina and extended shoreline.

That same shoreline formed a sizable segment of the perimeter of nearly every place I went during the first forty-four years of my life. Since an uncle lived in Michigan, driving around the lake's southern edge took us to an inexpensive vacation destination. When I went to college in Ohio, the interstates that hug the shoreline between

Milwaukee and Chicago made up nearly half my route (and more than half the time if Chicago traffic was particularly wretched). The graduate schools of my thirties were on either side of the lake—and I frequently visited my parents in metro Milwaukee.

The lake oriented my sense of direction. If I faced it, north was my left shoulder. When I moved to West Michigan and faced the lake, my right shoulder was north. (To be fair, I couldn't actually *see* "the big lake," as Michiganders call it, from where I lived; I couldn't see it from suburban Milwaukee either, but somehow I always knew where it was.) For twelve years I moved back and forth from one side of the lake to the other—my U-Haul unable to break the magnetic pull of the lake: Milwaukee to West Michigan to Madison and back to Michigan.

Then the colossal debacle at the seminary hurtled me across the country to the Edge of Nowhere. But even there, tucked between an ocean to the west and mountains to the east, I could still always find north.

Moving to Minnesota was a geographically jarring move. Life-long landmarks disappeared. No Great Lake near the Twin Cities. No mountains or ocean. In the absence of these, I got lost nearly every time I left home. I'd always had a keen sense of direction, managing perfectly well with my geographic landmarks and Rand McNally or maps printed from the internet, but from day one in my new surroundings, I had trouble finding my way around. On my travels from here to there by way of who-knows-where, I explored highways and side streets, neighborhoods and business districts. I drove in plenty of circles and backed out of lots of dead ends.

My disorientation was amplified by the fact that my apartment was situated upside-down in my mental orientation. On the map in my head, formed when I first explored my would-be home on the internet, the complex was located on the *north* side of Golden Valley Road. In the real world, it was on the *south* side. Every time I turned out of the parking lot, I went east or west—but felt like I was going *west* or *east*. It's no wonder I could barely find my way out of a cul-de-sac.

Without the boundaries of lake or ocean or mountain or even a skyscraper, I could not find north. Even when I studied a map, my brain would not stay fixed on the proper orientation of my apartment. Unable to recalibrate my mental compass, I could not get my directional bearings. I got lost so often because I didn't know where I had started. How could I possibly know where I was going? My sense of place spun like a broken compass.

But it wasn't just directional confusion and the disappearance of geographic landmarks that left me flailing. As I wrestled over the issues that had landed me in a dead-end job at midlife in Minnesota, I realized that other landmarks were also gone—theological ones.

Like topography, theology also shapes a life. Basic beliefs about who God is (and isn't) form landmarks that determine the directions we go or don't go. Every choice we make, whether or not we realize it, is rooted in what we believe about God's person and action, both in the larger world and in our personal spheres.

Some beliefs about God that had functioned as landmarks in my life had proved false. They would have been better called hypotheses, in need of more information to be embraced as truth. Since the long-ago walk when my dad had taught me the word *hypothesis*, I'd seen more of the world. I'd observed ideas in greater contexts and had time to reflect on their viability. I'd tested beliefs, albeit unwillingly, through my circuitous career path. Discovering that some could not hold up, I'd discarded them and tried again.

Three belief-hypotheses in particular could not explain where I found myself in life. They were inadequate to make sense of the evidence that lay shattered around me.

The first had to do with what I thought God wanted from me. I believed that in order to please God I needed to achieve my potential—that is, my *perceived* potential. To do anything less would be poor stewardship, a waste of the talents God had given me. From my childhood, Jesus's parable of the unfaithful servant who squandered his single "talent" had haunted me. I knew God had given me many more talents than just one—some of this knowledge was self-awareness, but plenty of people around me had affirmed it. My parents, teachers, and other loving adults often told me that God had gifted me with intelligence and creativity, that he had great plans for me, that they were excited to see how God would use me.

I am sure that such comments were only meant to encourage me, to cast a vision for what I might become. When I taught fifth graders, I said the same kinds of things—telling dear students they were capable, even gifted, and hoping my words would nourish them on their way through adolescence and into adulthood.

In the complex brew that creates a psyche, these words mixed with my drive to achieve and my pursuit of excellence. They blended with the perfectionism that dictated my conscience. And altogether, they resulted in the misguided belief that if I was able to do something, I should, and then I should also excel at it—and maybe even be the best. This was how I would hear the commendation that I longed for when I died: "Well done, good and faithful servant."

Like many hypotheses, this one had some truth to it. Surely God does gift us and equip us, and surely he does want us to serve him with everything we are and have. But the guilt that accompanied my failure to achieve or excel or "simply" keep his commands is not what he had in mind when he distributed gifts. To borrow from the words of Linus, the theologian-philosopher of the Peanuts gang, it was not God who laid the heavy burden of a great potential on me. In addition to abilities and experiences, God gifts us with grace and Sabbath and freedom. Finding the balance between all these is neither easy nor subject to formulaic five-step plans, a truth I am still sorting out.

A second belief-hypothesis that guided my life choices concerned what I assumed God would do when I did what he wanted. I believed that living wisely and following God would lead to "a good life," which I understood to be the life I expected: a family, a comfortable place to live, a meaningful occupation, and enough money to pay the bills. I came by this belief honestly: the Old Testament book of Proverbs is based, in part, on it. And much of the Old Testament seems to support it: obey God, and he will bless you.

In practice, this belief was not as crassly cause-and-effect as it sounds. I didn't think of God as dangling a carrot in front of me, luring me to obey him. Nor did I consider my careful choices an attempt to manipulate God, obligating him to secure my future happiness. At least not consciously. I *wanted* to please him. As best I knew how as a child and youth and young adult, I loved him, and so I wanted to make him happy . . . which takes me back to the belief-hypothesis about achieving my potential.

These two belief-hypotheses converged in a third belief that took shape during my years in seminary. I believed that God had called me to be an Old Testament professor. After a meandering journey through the elementary school classroom, the church office, and the Christian publishing house, I felt as if I finally understood God's specific call on my life: to teach the Bible in the classroom and also write about it for people in the pew. It seemed like the perfect tapestry for the multicolored threads of my life story, and I doggedly pursued its fulfillment through the long years of graduate school and hiring cycles.

The battering I'd received at the hands of search committees and school administrators had already severely challenged this belief about my calling, and moving to Minnesota was itself a sign that I had all but abandoned it. But the loss of this landmark still disoriented me. The only career God had put in its place was a poor substitute—requiring little of me besides sheer endurance. If God didn't want me to be a professor or even to use my gifts much at all, then why did he give them to me? It all seemed upside down—and I simply could not get my head around the idea that my non-career might be all he wanted.

As the vicious storm of reality swirled around these theological landmarks, I struggled to find my footing. For as long as I could remember, I had done my best to steward what God had given me, to please him, to serve him wholeheartedly. And yet all this scrupulous, virtuous living had landed me in a dimly lit apartment off the beaten career path, with dust gathering on a PhD for a career that refused to materialize. I didn't understand why God had closed off so many roads, why he didn't seem to want me to use my talents, why my life looked woefully different from what I had ever expected.

My belief-hypotheses couldn't explain what had happened to me. What is more, they had oriented me toward a destination that was, really, more about me than it was about God. For my entire life, I had wanted God to use me. And I had assumed that he wanted to. But my relentless attempts to achieve my potential and live wisely were two sides of the same coin, currency that paid with a fulfilling life of service for God. What I had thought to be God's desire for my life better reflected the American god of self-actualization than the God who revealed himself in Jesus Christ and called me to lose my life to save it, to take up my own cross to follow him.

I realized that it wasn't my circumstances that were upside down. It was my theological sense of direction. I needed to find north.

Thankfully, not every theological landmark had crumbled—or even sustained damage—and one that remained had the immovability of the Great Lake that had oriented so much of my life. If I could only keep my eyes fixed on it, the world would stop spinning around me.

I still believed that a good God was on the throne. He had everything under control, and I could trust him.

During my first two weeks in Minnesota, he seemed especially keen to remind me of this.

The first reminder was monetary. I had taken a pay cut when I moved, and despite my early optimism that the cost of living would be less in Minnesota, the difference was negligible. It would cost me nearly as much to live in the Twin Cities as it had on the West Coast. Worse, I had no way of knowing when or even if I might get a raise. Money was a constant source of anxiety. This concern began before I ever reached Minnesota, when the logistics of ending one lease and beginning another cost me an additional month's rent. That first evening when Suzy and I started unpacking my boxes, we quickly realized that the apartment had not been well cleaned. The paint was fresh, and the carpet and linoleum were new, but the cupboards and drawers were grimy. Every flat surface had to be scrubbed. When I later mentioned this to the management—who, despite appearances, had paid for cleaning services—they refunded me nearly a full month's rent. God had my financial worries under control. I could trust him.

The next reminder came on the second Sunday I attended my new church. Before my boxes were even unpacked, I had decided that I would go to church where Loralee's family went. They were, after all, the reason I had moved to the Twin Cities; it would be silly to hunt for a church when they already had one. On this particular week, I arrived a few minutes early and sat near the back of the sanctuary to wait for my friends. I busied myself reading the bulletin while strangers slowly filled the seats around me. When I saw a petite, smartly dressed woman sit a few feet away from me, I gave her a second glance.

As I told Loralee after the service, the woman looked like the daughter of the pastor who had married my parents fifty-nine years earlier. It was a preposterous thing to know, but it was true nonetheless.

The church where I grew up was also where my mom had grown up. She and my dad had met there when he moved to Milwaukee for college, and the pastor who married them, all told, served the church for thirty years. He and his wife raised their two daughters there.

By the time I arrived in the church nursery, that pastor and his family had moved on. But after three decades of ministry, they had many friends in the area and returned for visits on occasion. As the years went by, one of the daughters came to town often enough that I learned to recognize her from across the church lobby, though I never met her. Seemingly immune to the passage of time, she always looked the same—her straight, light hair cut short around her face. I had a vague idea that she lived—or at some point had lived—in Minnesota, but knew next to nothing else about her.

Despite what my eyes were telling me in church that morning, I was sure that the woman sitting three feet away could not be her. It was too far fetched: I move from the West Coast to Minnesota and land in a church pew with someone from my home church of a different denomination in Wisconsin? Right.

Then halfway through the service, I saw it. Propped near her feet was a canvas bag stuffed with pamphlets and papers, but the only paper I could read from where I sat said "The Gospel Hour Beacon, April, 1981."

I almost laughed out loud. *The Gospel Hour* was a radio program started by that beloved pastor of my home church. It aired every Sunday morning in Milwaukee for years, and in connection with it, the church published a little bulletin called "The Gospel Hour Beacon."

I don't think I heard another word of the service going on around me. I was too stunned—by the presence of the woman next to me and, more, by the thirty-four-year-old leaflet visible in her bag.

After church I turned to her and said, "I think I know you." She looked at me quizzically. "Joan Kermott?" I asked, using her maiden name. When her face registered surprise, I went on and said, "Wendy Widder," knowing my last name would instantly connect. It was her turn to be stunned. I reminded her of my parents' first names and my mom's maiden name, and I watched her face as a rich store of memories opened. We visited for several minutes, swapping names of people and places.

I suspect our serendipitous encounter surprised and cheered her—but for me, it was like drinking hot chocolate by the fire after hours in a bitter winter. The sweetness of meeting someone who shared a piece of my history in a place where I had none warmed me from head to toe.

I told Joan I had recognized her but thought it too crazy to be true. Then when I saw the "Gospel Hour Beacon" in her bag, I knew

I was right. She said she'd had that paper in her bag for several months. She'd come across it at home and wanted to share a poem in it with a friend at church.

Well, that's what she thought anyway. What really happened is that my tender Father knew I was lost and cold; he knew I was bruised and afraid. He used that yellowed church bulletin to remind me that I was tucked in his arms—safe from danger and close to his heart.

God's timely reminders lifted my eyes to the northward landmark of his sovereign goodness. They also steadied me enough to identify two other landmarks—two belief-hypotheses that better explained my circumstances than those I had discarded. They weren't unknown to me, but until I moved—or was moved—into terrain where they were more visible, I'd had no reason to chart my course by them. These landmarks are wilderness formations, more prominent for the barren landscape they define, and I began to notice them during my bleak sojourn on the West Coast.

In the desolation there, I had asked God for clarity. What did he want of me if he wasn't going to provide a way to use all the "talents" he had given me? What did he want to do with the experiences and training that had seemed so purposeful? Was it all for nothing—or at least for not much? Was my long-awaited and much-labored-for career over before it ever had a chance to begin?

As I had let the dream of a meaningful career die, the first landmark came into view. I realized that what God wanted from me was obedience. That was all. Whether I saw any tangible benefits was irrelevant. Those Old Testament promises of blessed obedience were given to Israelites living under the covenant made at Sinai. That old covenant was eclipsed by the new covenant inaugurated by Jesus, who frequently told his disciples that following him would lead to suffering.

And whether my wise choices yielded any gain was beside the point. The portrait of a wise and successful person in Proverbs is only part of the picture. Proverbs, a book of wisdom, is part of an ancient genre that encompassed more than the formulaic path to a good life. The book of Job is also a wisdom text, its dense and difficult poems a necessary counterbalance to the tidy aphorisms of Proverbs. Job's saga challenges the assumption that those who are righteous necessarily reap rewards. Job lost everything. Sure, at the end of the book he gains it back and then some. But the man lost ten children—there was no regaining all he'd lost. Presented with the challenge "Will you serve me for nothing?" Job said yes.

Admittedly, this theological landmark isn't eye-catching—few tourists have time for it. But at least it's clear. God wasn't asking me to figure out how to maximize my gifts, live up to my potential, or build a career. I had a job and owed my employer an honest day's work and a good attitude. I had coworkers and friends to whom I could show love. I had a church where I could serve. Sometimes obedience is more complicated, but sometimes it's our excuses that make it so.

A second landmark that the wilderness threw into sharp relief was my Destination. A journey, by definition, has a capital-D destination, the place to which the path leads and where it stops. For the Christian, this Destination is described in a variety of ways: heaven, the new earth, the sweet by-and-by. It's life forever with Jesus in a place where there are no more tears, sorrow, or suffering; a place where all has been made right for human flourishing.

But as my island-top hike had reminded me some years earlier, journeys are also full of small-d destinations—ministops and even side roads along the way. Regardless of its Destination, every journey is unique, the miles passing different destinations. Some have pavilioned rest areas, interesting side trips, and awe-inspiring scenery. Others have miles of tumbleweed, blazing sun, and an occasional gas station. In the journey of life, none of these destinations is where travelers stay—even if they want to.

I have known my Destination since childhood, and it has guided many of my life choices. But it hasn't always been easy to keep in view. In the fertile landscape of youth, a canopy of trees blocked my view and blankets of wildflowers diverted my attention. The road before me opened to endless destinations, and trying to decide which way to turn and where to linger occupied a lot of energy.

I'm quite sure the Mapmaker intends us to enjoy the journey he marks out. He himself delights in the details: Why does spring come in so many shades of green? Why do the colors of a sleeping octopus shift when it dreams, and why does an octopus dream at all? I'm also sure that God lays out a road with destinations to be embraced: his own Son learned a trade, had deep friendships, and cared for his mother's needs. God wants me to care about what he cares about—which is all of creation.

But caring about something is different from counting on it—for fulfillment, joy, success, meaning, and any number of other needs. For some of us, the destinations along the way may provide tastes and even sizable portions of these things. Still, they will never completely satisfy. For others of us, some of these lesser destinations will be full of disappointment and even heartbreak. They can also help us see the Destination more clearly.

Walking the road God lays before me means taking the long view, while also making the most of where I am. The journey leads to endless splendor and unmarred goodness, forever, but there is much beauty and delight in the present—even in the wilderness. What I was beginning to realize is that enjoying the destinations along the way is easier when I take them as they are—rather than expecting them to be something else.

I was learning this lesson just in time.

11

THE FORD

M y sister's high school Bible teacher advised her to attend a Christian college because it was how she would find a husband: "You have to go where the fish are." (As it turned out, she graduated with her bachelor's degree but no bachelor.)

I had spent much of my life "where the fish are"—Christian school, Christian college, a large and active singles ministry, and even seminary. Yet I'd barely had any nibbles, much less a catch. Over the years, friends had tried to matchmake me, but their plans always fell apart before I could even meet their intended. It had been almost laughable.

As time went on, I came to believe what a pastor friend once told me: "Wendy, only God can keep you single." He meant this as the sincerest of compliments, and I took it as such. For reasons I didn't understand, God wanted me to be on my own. I didn't know if this was his permanent plan, but I figured if he changed his mind, he was plenty capable of doing what needed to be done, whether I gave him much "help" or not. So I busied myself with the life I had instead of furiously trying to attain the one that eluded me.

Then came the life-sucking season in the Pacific Northwest. On a lonely holiday weekend (after I had tried and failed to find someone to share homemade raspberry pie with me), I ventured to the e-Harmony website just to see what all the fuss was about. A number of friends and acquaintances had found their spouses through online dating, and while I was happy for them, I had always refused to try it. Honestly, it felt like desperation to me. But I was desperate.

I think the website smelled fresh bait; there was an offer for a free four-day weekend. I locked my doors and pulled my blinds (figuratively speaking) and decided I had nothing to lose but a little time. I pecked my way through the massive personality test and waited to see which Prince Charmings would land in my inbox.

For the next four mornings, several prospective matches appeared. Russell in New Mexico corresponded with me for a couple days, but he wasn't interested in chatting beyond my free days. So much for that. Back to the real world.

Not too many weeks later, e-Harmony offered a three-month deal that amounted to about thirteen dollars per month. I thought, *Forty bucks? I'd easily spend that on something fun or something for the apartment.* So I forked out forty dollars for the "fun" of it.

It wasn't much fun. Some profiles made me roll my eyes, like the Match who said the most important thing he was looking for in a person was "someone fun, outgoing, ambitious, deep, loyal, affectionate, stylish, fashionable, girly. Someone who can jump into my arms and let me catch her, love her, hold her, listen to her, and be best friends with." When I told this to a married friend (whom I'd sworn to secrecy about my venture), she said, "In the real world, things like that only result in pulled muscles."

I forced myself to look past bad grammar and sloppy punctuation, but even then, plenty of profiles made me cringe. These were mostly littered with selfies that should only have been deleted, never distributed. It's bad enough to post a selfie taken over the bathroom counter; it's worse to post two. Or using the bathroom mirror so that the picture shows the photographer holding the camera (with the flash). Or five selfies in the same outfit but taken against different walls. The only thing such pictures told me is that there were good reasons these guys were not married.

Still other profiles made me scratch my head, like the Match who said, "I believe people should get to know each other the old fashion way." Me too, Match. Me too.

But I pressed on. Trying to make the most of my investment, I initiated contact with about a dozen guys. Only one responded. I kept trying, eventually managing a handful of brief interactions with different matches—but none lasted long or went far.

Alan in Oklahoma asked me how my sexuality and sexual expression had impacted my life and past relationships. I was surprised by this question and thought it a bit invasive for early correspondence but decided to give him the benefit of the doubt; online dating is a strange medium. I told him I'd never been married and had lived within God's guidelines for sexual expression—so didn't have much to say. He quickly apologized, not realizing I hadn't been married (which meant, among other things, that he hadn't read my profile very carefully).

Ted from Colorado asked to skip the canned questions provided by e-Harmony and move to personal messages. He disappeared after one exchange. I have no idea what I said that sent him running. I suppose he could've googled me and found something that didn't appeal to him. (Goodness knows, I perfected my internet stalking skills by hunting down matches using only first names, occupations, cities, and whatever useful details I could find in their profile pictures.)

Bradley lived within two hours of the Edge of Nowhere. He sounded incredibly normal, and we corresponded for about a week—long enough for me to realize, as my sworn-to-secrecy friend noted, that "he does kind of go on and on . . . and on . . . and on . . ." He rambled down rabbit trails, ranted about pet peeves, and even sermonized—thankfully about things in his own life, not mine. It wasn't that I necessarily disagreed with everything he said, but I definitely got tired of reading it. When my friend said, "Yeah, that would get tiring in person," I said, "It's tiring in email."

I was almost relieved when my three months were over, agreeing with the assessment of George in *You've Got Mail* when his female colleague asked if he was online (by which she meant dating): "Well, as far as I'm concerned, the Internet is just another way of being rejected by women."[4] Amen, George.

In the midst of this nonsense, I gave several dozen longtime friends official permission to play matchmaker. No one took me up on it—except a friend in Argentina who had a Swedish guy in mind. That all got a little too complicated for me to be very interested. I suppose by the time I got around to asking for help, my friends were out of practice or, more likely, out of ideas.

I had not included my seminary friend Rhonda in this initial request for help—but not out of neglect. We had all but lost touch over the years, our contact limited to the occasional Christmas card.

Rhonda and I had worked together on a group project for a class we both detested. Our group of four was easily the best part of the class. She and I became walking buddies for the next year or so until she and her husband moved out of state.

In the blur of my move to Minnesota, I had forgotten that Rhonda and Ben lived in the Twin Cities. A few weeks after I limped into town, she saw on Facebook that I was in the area and messaged me an invite for dinner with her family. On one hand, I was happy to reconnect. On the other hand, I didn't know if I was up to it. Rhonda is intense and extroverted. She is staunchly feminist, and nothing pushes her buttons like injustice. I knew that reconnecting would mean telling her where I'd been for the last few years and how the heck I ended up in her neighborhood. I was certain that my stories about our alma mater and about Dr. Eastwood's school would infuriate her, and I had no energy left for fury. My wounds were still fresh, and spending the evening explaining them sounded painful and exhausting.

But friends are friends, and I needed every one I could get in my new surroundings. Besides, she lived only two and a half miles past Loralee's house. My chances of getting lost were low.

As expected, Rhonda did ask for all the details, and she seethed over the injustices. More than that, though, she grieved with me. She extended the compassion and empathy of a friend—as I should have known she would. I enjoyed a lovely meal with her family on their deck. Just before dessert, her face lit up, and turning to me she said, "We should introduce you to—" then she cast a glance at her husband, as if for permission to continue.

I answered for him. "Rhonda, several years ago I gave my friends permission to matchmake me. You can introduce me to anyone you think I should meet."

Rick was a deacon at the little church she and Ben were attending. She told me what little she knew about him. He was from Iowa and spent many weekends there helping his widowed mom. Rhonda said he was an electrical engineer and that he'd been married when he lived in California some years earlier—but his wife had left him. No kids.

I took what little information she gave me and got to work googling. Rick's digital footprint was smaller than a baby bootie, but I managed to find his mom on Facebook—at least I was pretty sure it was his mom. I scrolled through her pictures, which were mostly of beaming grandchildren, but a recent family picture stretched across the top of her home page. It wasn't hard to find the single guy in the back corner. Clean cut in a striped polo shirt and cargo shorts, he had deep-set eyes and a bright smile. His blond hair was cut short, but there was enough of it to make him look younger than the forty to forty-four years old Google said he was.

Meanwhile, Rhonda wasted no time. She approached Rick at church that weekend and, finding him agreeable, gave him my number. He called on Tuesday night. We awkwardly introduced ourselves and even more awkwardly tried to set up our own blind date—no small feat when you want to make a good impression but have no idea what the other person likes. We finally settled on a plan for the following Tuesday afternoon: we would meet for coffee, drive to a historic park along the Mississippi River for a walk, and then maybe get something to eat.

Tuesday afternoon is an odd time for a date, but Rick said he didn't work on Tuesdays. Since I set my own hours, I could arrange to have the afternoon off. I didn't really understand his work schedule—he said he worked three or four days of twelve-hour shifts and then had a couple days off. It seemed like strange hours for an electrical engineer—though why I thought I knew what an engineer's schedule should be escapes me.

I had low expectations. Rick had seemed nice enough on the phone, but as I told Loralee, he sounded blue-collar—a comment I quickly followed with "There's nothing wrong with being blue-collar, but, well, I'm not." The saddle on my high horse was well worn. (Blue-collar workers make the world go round, while a whole lot of white-collar folks just talk about it; but still, I couldn't fathom how we'd be a good match.) Besides his strange-to-me schedule, Rick's manner of speaking was folksy. He didn't speak with a drawl, but he seemed to think with one—that is, his thoughts stretched out like a long vowel in search of a final consonant.

Loralee reminded me that it was a low-risk date. The worst that could happen is I'd have a dreadful time and never have to see him again. And maybe, just maybe, it wouldn't be that bad, and I'd at least gain a new friend.

The Caribou Coffee shop where we agreed to meet was in a nearby mall. I arrived early, giving myself plenty of time to scope things out before Rick arrived. Caribou's location was ideal for my purposes: a first-floor kiosk in full view of a second-floor overlook. I settled on an upstairs bench, nibbled on a protein bar, and watched for someone resembling the polo-shirt-cargo-shorts guy I'd seen on Facebook.

When he sauntered into view, wearing cargo shorts and a different polo shirt, I made my way to the escalator. The mall was not crowded, so it wasn't hard for him to realize the woman walking toward him must be me. We introduced ourselves, and Rick said, "Did you want some coffee? Or not?"

I definitely wanted coffee, and since he'd indicated on the phone that he would pay for dinner, I asked if I could get the coffee. I told him, truthfully, that a friend had given me a gift card—because somehow, to me at least, that eased the potential discomfort of the offer.

Coffee in hand, we headed to his car, a cream-colored Chrysler that was much nicer than my almost-bare-bones, stick-shift Elantra. It wasn't new, but it was spotless, the cleanest car I'd ever been in that wasn't on a dealer's lot. I settled in for the fifteen-minute drive to the park, where Rick found a parking space and plugged the meter.

We set off walking. Neither of us had been to the park before, so we simply wandered wherever there were sidewalks or trails. Walking makes talking easier, and our conversation ambled along with us. We covered predictable territory for two people who've just met: families, backgrounds, jobs, and hobbies. Rick was to his family what my brother is to ours: the second-oldest only son of four children. And his dad, like mine, had taught fifth grade. His mom had been an elementary school teacher before Rick's older sister came along, and then she stayed home to raise a family. Our upbringings had been similarly conservative, with attending church almost a more frequent activity than watching television.

It was a humid ninety-degree day, so after a couple hours on our feet, we found a bench near the pavilion. Rick asked if I wanted ice cream. I was dog-tired and drenched with sweat—ice cream would have been wonderful—but since I thought we'd be having dinner soon, I said no. While we sat, he asked what brought me to Minnesota—a loaded question if ever there was one. With enough detail to make the point but not so much as to overwhelm him, I explained that I'd been unsuccessful trying to find a teaching job and had been miserable on the West Coast. I'd moved to the Twin Cities to start over, and I was waiting for God to put together whatever it was he wanted me to do next.

We walked a bit more and finally decided it was time to call it a day. We returned to his car, and he drove me back to my car at the mall without saying anything about dinner. It was 6:30 and I was starving (I typically ate at 5:00), but not knowing what happened to the dinner plan, I said nothing. When I got out of the car, I said I'd had a nice time and thanked him.

"Well, you paid for everything!" he said, as if to question what I was thanking him for.

I protested, "No! My friend did! And you paid for parking!"

He laughed. "That was only three dollars!"

First dates—and blind ones at that—are unavoidably awkward.

Mystified about the dinner that wasn't, I stopped at Smashburger on the way home. Did I misunderstand? Was he so exhausted after four hours in the sweltering heat that he just wanted to go home? Was it a bad date and who wants to get dinner? Was he offended that I "paid" for the coffee?

Later that evening, I reported to Loralee. "It was fine. We had a nice time, but I don't see this going anywhere."

When I saw Rhonda a few days later, she wanted the scoop. I told her the same thing, including the strange business about dinner.

"What! He didn't feed you?"

When she saw him at church on Sunday and asked how things went, he said he'd had a nice time. She persisted, "Why didn't you take her to dinner?"

He said he thought I just wanted to go home since I kept saying how hot it was—and, I learned later, since I'd already declined his offer for ice cream.

He called the next day to see if I wanted to go out for dinner.

During the fall months, we kept going out—walks in other local parks, the theater, holiday concerts, dinner. It was nice to have a reason to do things I wouldn't ordinarily do and a person with whom to do them, but the ambivalence in my reports to Loralee didn't change. I always had a good enough time to go again, but I still didn't see a future for us.

It wasn't that I doubted he was a great guy. When cancer had taken his dad a decade earlier, Rick left a job he loved in California and moved back to the Midwest within an easy drive of his mom. He took a sizable pay cut for a job he never liked so he could help her navigate the devastating terrain of early widowhood. Two of his sisters lived close by, but both were in the all-consuming season of early parenting. Since Rick had no such attachments, he decided to take responsibility for many of their mom's needs in those years. There was plenty of yard work and an endless stream of odd jobs—not to mention, he was good company in her unwanted and still-new solitude. He bought a camper to upgrade the one his parents had used, and then he bought a truck to pull it. His family's lifelong camping tradition continued because Rick stepped into his dad's role.

Five years after he'd returned, his mom had settled into new routines. When Rick's former employer called with an offer to work in the Twin Cities office—a four-hour drive from Iowa—he took it. He still spent more weekends than not traveling home to be available to help and to spend time with his family.

The church in the Twin Cities that he and Rhonda's family attended was small, and that was one of the main reasons he chose it. He valued being an active church member, and knowing how easy it is to get lost in a large congregation—especially as a single person—he joined a small one for the accountability of being involved.

I liked him, and I respected him, but he was not the kind of person I had always thought I would marry—that is, if I ever got married. As a child, I had dreamed of marrying a pastor. Then I was sure my match would be someone who shared my college memories or perhaps someone I met at my home church. After I went to seminary, I assumed a potential spouse would have a similar theological education. Then as I accumulated more graduate degrees, I figured my only prospects would be in the academic world. As a writer and editor, I was pretty sure anyone without strong language skills would drive me to insanity.

Rick fit none of these expectations. He had a bachelor's degree in the field of engineering; numbers were his thing, not words. While he had grown up in a strong Christian environment and graduated from a Christian high school, his denomination and interests were different enough from mine that our Christian circles barely intersected. He knew Billy Graham and Max Lucado but had never heard of John Piper or Dwight L. Moody.

I didn't see how we'd ever find enough in common to make a long-term relationship work. But I wasn't willing to give up yet—after all, he was the one door that God hadn't yet shut. I couldn't *not* walk through it. And I knew I had accumulated layers of expectations by midlife that may or may not be valid. As I told Loralee, Rick's biggest problem was that he was a real person.

Well, there was one other thing. In all the time we'd spent together, he had never brought up his ex-wife or even hinted that there was a story to tell me someday. It was as if she had never existed. For me, it became the elephant in the room. How can you date someone for several months and not say a word about such a significant season of life?

My friends had their theories about Rick's silence, but the one that seemed to make the best sense of a strange situation came from a friend with a counseling degree. She said Rick had all the marks of someone who'd been badly hurt. I'm sure she told me what those identifiers were, but all I remember is the bottom line: it was probably going to take awhile for him to trust me with something so painful. I needed to be patient.

By mid-December, my patience had run out. I needed him to talk to me, and I especially needed to know what he was thinking about us. One way or another, we were going to have this conversation.

The Saturday before Christmas, he invited me to his house to see his lights. The man loved Christmas lights, hanging countless strands on his own house, his mother's house, and even on his neighbor's house. We planned to go for a walk on neighborhood trails, have dinner, and maybe play a board game.

This was to be my first visit to his space. I'd had him to my apartment twice—six weeks earlier for slow-cooker beef burgundy after a matinee and then just that week for take-and-bake pizza before we went to a comedy club. The first time I'd thought awkward—expecting him, surrounded by All Things Wendy, to ask questions about this, that, or the other. But he didn't. Maybe he was just taking it all in? The second time I was days removed from a mini-meltdown—the closest the Edge had been in several years—and I had dared to tell him about it. While he had listened, he hadn't said much in return—though I wasn't sure what I thought he should say.

On the designated afternoon I drove the forty-five minutes to his house, and I fretted the entire way, trying to figure out how to start the conversation I needed to have. When I arrived he gave me the grand tour of his house, which he'd had built when he moved to the area. I was surprised by how nice it was—I hadn't expected a bachelor's place to be so well decorated. As I looked around, I couldn't help but think, *That's exactly the woodwork/cabinets/color I would have picked.* The scented candle burning on the kitchen island was a nice touch too.

We bundled up for a walk and headed to the nature preserve that bordered his neighborhood. Before we'd gone too far, he grabbed my hand—a first. I thought, *Okay, good. This is going the right direction for The Conversation.* I decided to ask his thoughts about what I'd said the other night—about my struggle with panic and anxiety. He said he didn't really know what to say, except that he felt bad that I had to go through that.

Well, that didn't go far. For a while we chatted about work and local news. We circled around the playground and headed across a little bridge. I kept trying to find a way to get him to talk about "us"—and more importantly, about "her"—but mostly he said things like "I'm a guy. I don't have that much to say." This was going splendidly.

A bit farther along, he suddenly stopped. Turning to face me, he looked me in the eyes and said, "Well, you beat me to the awkward conversations." He paused, and I panicked. *Is he going to propose? Gah! No!* Without saying another word, he leaned over and kissed me.

My brain froze, but my body moved. My face slid away, nose to his shoulder, and my arms grabbed him in a hug. He hugged back as I wailed, "You can't do that if you're not going to talk to me." And there we stood. Neither of us moved for ten solid minutes. A couple times I asked, "Are you cold?" or something equally inane, and he said, "No."

I had no idea what had just happened, much less have any words for it, and the man of few words was happy to stand there holding me. At least I hadn't run away?

Knowing one of us had to do something and also suspecting my tolerance for inaction was lower than his, I finally said in his ear, "Well, I guess we can't stand here like this forever." I think he laughed.

We stepped back, I took his hand, and we resumed walking. What followed was the conversation I'd agonized over all week and had been trying for thirty minutes to manufacture with my awkward questions. His kiss, while shocking to me, was much more effective. I decided that a good place to start was to talk about our previous relationships. That seemed a sure way to address the ex-wife elephant in the room.

He began. "Well, there's not much to say." I could see this was not going to go well.

He continued, telling me he'd had two girlfriends over the years and dated a couple women here and there. He talked a little about the girlfriends—one in California years earlier and the other in South Dakota. But none of his words registered in my head. I was stuck on where his ex-wife fit into this "not much to say" monologue.

And then he was done. *Okay,* I told myself, *I guess I have to just ask.*

"So, this is awkward—but I thought you had been married . . ." My voice trailed off.

"What? Why?!" Either he was an amazing actor or he was truly stunned.

"And," I dared to finish, "divorced."

"Why would you think that?" he practically sputtered.

I told him that's what Rhonda had said, to which he responded, "Why would *she* think that? Is that what everyone at church thinks?"

Of course, I had no answer for that. I had no answer for anything—except suggesting that if he were going to puke, as seemed a real possibility from the look on his face, he could do it under that tree over there.

We kept walking, now both of us confused. I recounted my own relationship history, not terribly exciting on a good day but especially dull in light of what had just happened.

For another hour we followed the trails wherever they went and talked about "us." Dating and beyond at midlife is fundamentally different than it is in earlier decades, and before we had met each other, neither of us had reason to ponder these differences. As we mused aloud about the colossal changes associated with merging two established lives, we both acknowledged reservations. We also learned that, after almost four months of seeing each other, neither of us had told our families anything. For me, it was mostly a matter of not wanting to do damage control if and when the relationship didn't work; for him, it was a matter of not wanting the third degree about something he wasn't entirely sure of.

When we got back to his house, we played several rounds of Dutch Blitz and then had dinner. By that time, the import of our ninety-minute talk was catching up with me, and it was my turn to feel sick. I swallowed enough spoonfuls of soup to keep my cover, thankful for a meal that didn't require much chewing. Then we watched a movie before calling it a night. On my way out the door, I hugged him (briefly this time) and said, "So, this has been A LOT to take in. It's going to take me a while to process it." We were both headed to our respective families for Christmas, and I, for one, needed the time away.

I punched in Loralee's phone number before I had turned off Rick's street. I waited for her to answer, hoping it wasn't time to put the kids to bed because I really needed to talk to her. She picked up.

"Ohmyword! Ohmyword! Ohmyword!" I yelled into the phone.

"Wen! Are you all right? Are you safe? Where are you?"

"Yes, yes, I'm fine. I'm on my way home from Rick's. OH MY WORD."

My head was exploding, and it didn't take long to make hers do the same. For the entire drive home (during which I made a few wrong turns and had to put the phone down until I could retrace my route), I told her in torrents about the day. Then when I got home, my fingers flew through the story in online chats with a friend on the East Coast and another on the West Coast. Before the night was over, heads were exploding in three time zones. (The only friend whose head didn't explode was Rhonda, who upon hearing about the day's events said, "Well, you finally have something real to talk about!" and that they must have had Rick mixed up with someone else at church.)

The real problem wasn't the misinformation about Rick's marital status. That alone would have been good news to someone like me who also had never been married, not to mention the relief that he wasn't keeping his divorce a secret. (As my West Coast friend said, "That makes me feel way better about him not bringing up his divorce, since it didn't happen!") The problem was the persona I had constructed around him, based on my friend's assessment that he had been deeply hurt and needed time to build trust. Much of my perception of him was framed and then fed by a massive misunderstanding. So on top of trying to sort out what was in my head from the unexpected kiss, I also had to "put Rick back together" in my head—reconfiguring a whole lot of erroneous thinking from the past several months.

As I wrestled with why "the real Rick" hadn't talked about his feelings, a married friend said, "Wendy, he sounds like a normal guy to me." Another friend who was married to a quiet man agreed. They both said the solution was time. No one likes to be put on the spot to share their feelings. I needed to give Rick time—not to trust me, necessarily, but to find the ways to talk that felt natural to him.

I also continued to be haunted by my expectations of what a relationship should be like, what Rick should be like, and how I should feel about all of it. I wondered if he had enough ambition for me. For as long as I could remember, I'd been working toward the Next Thing, making a plan to accomplish whatever it was I wanted to do (or what I thought God wanted me to do). One night, in search of Rick's goals, I asked where he saw himself in five years or what he hoped for out of the second half of his life. He paused, then said, "I hope it's as blessed as the first half has been."

Hmph. I had to admit that was actually a pretty good answer.

All my go-to girlfriends were either single or had married young. While they were keen voices of sanity, it was the perspective of my uncle and aunt that steadied me when I needed it most. Having married later in life, they understood the strange terrain I was stumbling through. When I asked my uncle for his thoughts about expectations versus reality, he responded by talking about the wonderful gift of companionship. He said relationships were messy, and they were a lot of work, but the reward was in all that work. He and my aunt agreed that Rick sounded normal and that how I was feeling sounded spot on too.

One friend had suggested that Rick and I read a book together, thinking it might prompt the kind of deeper conversation I was looking for. I've always gone to books for answers, so that seemed like a good idea to me. Rick's response was lukewarm, but he didn't refuse, so I started hunting down the right resource. Nothing jumped off my shelves, and not knowing the genre of relationship resources very well, I stalled out.

He and I texted over the holidays and chatted on the phone when we both got back to town. I had sent him a long email processing our last date, but I knew we needed the right time and place to talk about it. We made plans for dinner and a movie on New Year's Eve, and Rick as much as said we'd talk then.

I expected that we'd talk over dinner, and I was prepared with a mental list once he initiated the conversation. But he didn't. Instead, we caught up on our holidays at home and small-talked about our surroundings. On our way from the car to the theater, he finally brought it up. He said he'd appreciated my letter, and paraphrasing some of it, he said with a laugh, "I don't want to make your head explode, but I think we've moved to the next level." Like me, however, he wasn't exactly sure what that meant. He said he'd thought about me a lot while he was home for Christmas. Then he reached for the door to the theater and followed me in.

Is that it? All my uncertainties about our compatibility rushed back. My stomach knotted, and my brain raced along familiar ruts.

Looking back, I have no idea what I expected him to say, what script I wanted him to follow. But I am prone to put a lot of stock in words, and he hadn't given me many to work with. Still, I did plenty of overthinking with what he had said. Mostly, I wanted to know how the story turned out—which, of course, he couldn't know. Sometimes I felt like I had to end it. Other times it seemed like a little voice was saying, "Steady on. One step at a time." Knowing whether the voice was God's or that of my untrustworthy emotions was not always clear.

Rick came into my life at what was both the worst and best time possible. I had moved to Minnesota with nothing but ashes of dreams. I was broken and empty and wounded. My career had been aborted, and my job was its ugly stepsister. From where I sat in my dark apartment every day, looking at work I loathed, I couldn't fathom a future. I was desperate for God to do something.

Desperation is a terrible reason to date someone. Yet it was my hopelessness—apart from God's work—that kept me going out with a guy who may not have gotten my attention at earlier times in my life. No, he wasn't a lot of what I expected, but he was a man of integrity and hard work, love for God and neighbor, commitment and contentment, gentleness and humility. I suspected that my reservations were less about him than they were about me and the uncomfortable requirements that come with close relationships—things like dying to self, acknowledging sin, and swallowing pride.

And so I swung back and forth between wanting to call it quits and looking forward to going out again.

Then something happened.

The day after our New Year's Eve date, I was in the blue-blackness of my old friend, the Edge, made worse by my Rick angst. For myself more than anyone else, I wrote a blog post called "Steady On, 2016." It was a general piece about my midlife battle with shattered expectations and the ongoing difficulty of reshaping dreams. My conclusion was that moving forward only happened in the daily decision to get out of bed and choose to follow God down whatever path he put before me that day, to go wherever it led. It was, I said, the journey of discipleship.

A friend who read the post said it reminded her of a book by pastor-author Eugene Peterson, *A Long Obedience in the Same Direction*. The book came out in 1980 and was reprinted in 2000, so there were plenty of used copies on Amazon. A fan of anything from Peterson, I promptly ordered one.

The next day, Saturday, I emailed a few friends and, among other things, asked them to pray that God would let me love Rick—and if he didn't, I needed him to make it really clear that I needed to let Rick go. I liked Rick a great deal, but love—at least as anything more than a conscious choice—seemed out of reach. I told my friends that it would be a privilege to love him.

On Sunday afternoon, I called Rick to see if he wanted company for the Packers-Vikings game that night. Of course he did—and why didn't I just come for dinner too? Having nothing to do at home, I went plenty early. To pass the extra time, we read through some letters his parents had sent him during his Navy days. He was compiling the twenty-five-year-old collection into scrapbooks to give his mom for Mother's Day, knowing how much she'd enjoy reliving their history. Going through the letters was a delightful window into his family and his past, but despite having a good time, I couldn't escape the nagging thoughts: *This just isn't going to work. He's a super nice guy, but we have such different personalities and ways of thinking.* I was sure I needed to call the whole thing off. But how? What real reason could I even give?

When dinner was ready, we moved to the kitchen table, which had nothing on it yet except two books he'd received for Christmas. One I had given him—about the Packers-Vikings rivalry. The other stunned me: *A Long Obedience in the Same Direction.*

I stared at it, finally asking, "Where did you get this?"

He said his pastor had given it to him for Christmas.

I didn't tell Rick what I was thinking—that whatever my doubts and reservations might be, it seemed pretty clear that God had, at the very least, said, "Don't quit yet." Later that week I emailed him the suggestion that we read and discuss Peterson's book together. When he responded, "That could be an idea. We will have to discuss on how to discuss . . . ," I laughed. If we never did anything with the book, it would be okay. I suspected it had already accomplished what God wanted it to. Steady on, 2016.

THE LABYRINTH

The forecast of barely seventy degrees was cool for a midsummer day. Clouds would move in later, but when I set out in shorts and a light sweatshirt just after breakfast, the breeze was light and the sun was on its steep morning incline. My destination was the Mount Olivet Retreat Center, a twenty-minute drive through the outskirts of the Twin Cities. My backpack lay on the passenger seat, mostly for the water bottle inside, along with directions scrawled on scrap paper.

It was July of 2020, and I was off to complete a homework assignment for an online class, an eight-week course on spiritual formation. Not only was 2020 a rough year the world over, it had been another tough year for me. My dad had been in decline for some time before COVID-19 circled the globe, and he died six weeks into the worldwide shutdown. His death, while a mercy, came at what felt like the worst possible time in his long life. The pandemic robbed him (his loved ones, really) of the proper, public goodbye he deserved for a life well lived. At the same time, my newly bereaved mom was trapped in a yearlong lockdown at her assisted-living facility. Because her computer ability was limited, she was accessible only by phone and through her first-floor apartment window. I'd lost my dad and the healing that comes from communal grief, and my mom seemed impossibly far out of reach.

My professional angst also continued as I flailed about trying to cobble together some kind of meaningful career identity for all my years of academic labor. I no longer worked full-time for the West Coast digital media company. Instead, I was an independent contractor, picking up freelance writing and editing gigs as well as occasional speaking engagements.

In search of some fresh help navigating life as it was, I contacted a spiritual director I'd met through Loralee and Kyle and asked about one-on-one sessions. She said she was offering a class that might be a good fit for me—and it included three free individual sessions in spiritual direction. Always one to snatch more bang for my Dutch buck, I signed up for the course.

When she offered a second course at a deep discount, I registered for it too; the Dutch gene is strong. The class included reading Teresa of Avila's *The Interior Castle*, which I learned is a classic guide for spiritual development. St. Teresa, who lived in the 1500s, was a Spanish nun and Christian mystic. This alone made me squirm—not that she was a nun but that she was a mystic.

Mysticism was not something I knew much about, except that it was "out there" and was practiced in religions that dealt in esoteric experience more than reasoned theology. My branch of Baptist had its own emphasis on experience—a "Jesus and me" approach that sometimes eschewed accountability for personal beliefs and practices—but it knew nothing of the ecstatic rapture Paul described to the Corinthians when he said he was "caught up to the third heaven . . . whether in the body or apart from the body" where he "heard inexpressible things" (2 Cor. 12:2–4 NIV). Besides my own church background, a decade of graduate school in biblical and theological studies had reinforced any discomfort I already had about Christian mysticism.

Trekking through seminary and then the program in Madison had challenged, in good ways, the foundations of what I believed and how I understood God. My studies had transformed my perspectives and my thinking process. The takeaway value of that education was enormous, and I've never regretted it.

However, it didn't come without some collateral damage—primarily, a self-righteous sense of "how to do the Bible" and "how to do Christianity" and "how to do a relationship with God." What it all boiled down to was this: use your head. Sure, I knew this wasn't all there is, that we are more than heads. But for ten years I awoke every day knowing that my academic survival depended on marshaling all my mental forces for combat. The enemy was anything that smacked of subjectivity or that couldn't be footnoted with peer-reviewed sources (the standard for credible research).

But by 2020—far removed from the academy, abused and all but abandoned by it—I was seeking a corrective for my ingrained approach to the Bible and even God himself. Grad school had given me a lot of answers, and it had taught me how to ask good questions, but that wasn't enough. I desperately needed—and *wanted*—balance that respected my head but involved my heart as well. My studies had cut me off from ways of thinking and spiritual practices that the church had embraced for much of its existence. Taking this class, this introduction to Christian mysticism, was a way to tiptoe into that world, to baby-step into another way of knowing God.

The homework assignment I was completing on that July morning was to walk a labyrinth. A labyrinth is a pattern marked on the ground—typically in grass, pavement, or brick. Its perimeter is a circle, and inside the circle a single path winds to the center. Unlike a maze, the path has no obstacles or dead ends; it goes one and only one way. "Walking the labyrinth" involves stepping onto the path at the circle's edge and slowly moving to the center, all the while praying and reflecting. The center is a place to enjoy resting in God's presence before beginning the journey out again.

I had first heard of walking a labyrinth a few months earlier. A friend had recommended a book about spiritual practices that have been part of the church (though never my particular churches) for centuries. In the chapter on labyrinths, the author had anticipated my discomfort and even objections when she noted that labyrinths make some Christians nervous because they are also used in traditions that aren't Christian. But, as she said, the labyrinth itself is not inherently mystical; its purpose in Christian tradition is to provide an opportunity for reflective prayer.

I was skeptical I'd find much value in the exercise. Furthermore, I even *resisted* thinking it would have any effect because I was sure I'd be disappointed if I approached it with expectations. However, never one to ignore a homework assignment, I'd hunted down a labyrinth in the Twin Cities metro, delighted to find one relatively close by. At least doing my homework wouldn't take half the day. As I left home that morning, I reminded myself that some highly educated, highly respected friends would consider the practice valuable. My nod to their opinion was to ask God to meet me in the labyrinth, despite my doubts.

When I arrived at the retreat center, the parking lot was nearly empty. It was the peak of shutdowns, so I wasn't surprised to see few cars. I'd made my reservation online and assumed that, upon my arrival, I would check in and be pointed toward the labyrinth. I parked in the center of the lot and followed Main Office signage to a nearby building.

The doors were locked, and the lights were off. *Hmm. I guess I'll just wander around and look for the labyrinth—how hard can it be to find?*

A wood-chip path led from the sidewalk to the woods. Seeing a sign posted near the trees, I followed the trail to read it. It was a map of the grounds, but nothing on the map indicated where the labyrinth was. *Hmph.*

It seemed unlikely that I needed to go farther along the path into the woods; I expected that the retreat center wanted attendees to have easy access to the labyrinth. So I turned back, left the path, and headed across the lawn toward a grassy knoll. I could see another path that meandered into the tall grasses and wildflowers of a field where a cross stood. That seemed like a good place for a meditative walk.

As I crossed the dew-damp grass, my sandal straps rubbed against my wet feet. Undeterred, I resolved to enjoy the lovely summer morning and kept moving. When I reached the cross, I found a couple of benches but no labyrinth. Another grassy expanse opened up farther down the path, so I followed the trail for a few more steps—until again concluding that a labyrinth so far away would not be very usable.

Pausing to drink from my water bottle, I turned around and headed back toward the complex of buildings, which included the chapel. That seemed like a logical place for a spiritual experience, but alas, the labyrinth was not there either. I walked toward another clearing—where, in a different season, skiers would have started their course around the grounds. I wasn't surprised to come up empty one more time.

On one hand, I was frustrated. How hard could it possibly be to find a labyrinth? And why weren't there any signs? On the other hand, the irony of the situation was obvious. I was lost *looking* for the labyrinth. It seemed a fitting metaphor for my lifelong pursuit of what I thought God had called me to. I'd traveled to one place, then another, then another, all while trying to reach that small-*d* destination of God's calling. And despite all my hard-fought efforts, it remained elusive.

Or most of it, anyway. At least one aspect of what God wanted for me had become very clear since the murkiness of my early 2016 blog post four and a half years earlier.

In the weeks following God's gentle "Don't quit yet" encouragement, dating became a bit more comfortable. I was able to focus on enjoying Rick for who he was rather than who he wasn't. We spent

189

long winter evenings reading through the rest of his Navy letters. When the weather allowed, we went for walks, often followed by dinner at local restaurants. At a winter carnival, I recruited a passerby to take our first picture together. I started to think in terms of "us" instead of "me" and "him."

One evening Rick came to my apartment with his mind set on fixing things. My alarm clock was giving me trouble, my heat register was clanking (despite the grumpy maintenance man's half-hearted puttering), and my antenna TV refused me more than one channel. While I looked on, Rick fussed with the TV and tinkered with the register. He adjusted my alarm clock settings and promised to remind me to turn it off on nights before I wanted to sleep in. When I asked if I'd ruined the cord on my yogurt maker, he took it home to fix. The last person so devoted to my small comforts had been my dad. Rick's tenderness made me feel vulnerable and loved all at once.

Bouts of panic and uncertainty didn't magically disappear, but my uncle, aunt, and friends were at the ready to talk me through. Loralee liked to remind me that I didn't have to reserve the church; I just had to decide whether I wanted to go out with Rick again. And I always did.

I told Rick that each step we took forward in our relationship felt like wearing a new pair of shoes that pinched. I had to walk in them for a while before they became comfortable. Then, as soon as that pair got comfortable, I was asked to trade them for another pinching pair. He said he thought about the new stages like he did a trip to the dentist: just get it over with; the discomfort is brief, and then it's done. I wished I could trade my new shoes for his dentist.

Numerous questions cluttered each step forward for me. Rick patiently listened to my suggestions for sorting out whatever was on my mind—solutions that usually involved reading books—but he didn't seem to be bothered by the things I was. My uncle assured me that, even in this ongoing struggle, Rick and I sounded normal. He said finding middle ground would take conversation, patience, and forbearance. And still many issues would never be completely resolved—or even be resolvable.

By Valentine's Day, we agreed it was time to tell our families. I told mine via a long email, which I wrote and sent at 5:30 the next morning. Then I talked to my parents on the phone later in the day and answered emails from my siblings. Rick, on the other hand, had long been plotting how he would tell his family. Two weeks after I sent my email, he went to Iowa for a family dinner, and after the leisurely meal, he told his mom she needed to set an extra plate the next time he came home. Then he sat back and enjoyed the show.

With the word out, we made back-to-back weekend trips to Wisconsin and then to Iowa to meet each other's families. After our first whirlwind trip, we got into Rick's car for the drive back to Minnesota. He turned the key in the ignition, looked at me, and said, "How do your new shoes feel?" I told him they felt pretty good. The next weekend we took our second quick trip, and my pinching shoes got a little more comfortable.

As we drove out of Rick's hometown, we talked about how nice it had been to visit our families and finally feel like we had someone to belong to. I asked if he still had any reservations about us. He didn't and asked if I did. I said no. Some months earlier, I'd made myself a list of all the conversations I thought we needed to have, all the things we needed to work through as a couple. But when I'd looked at the list not too many days earlier, I realized that nothing left on it was a deal breaker. Nothing was urgent, and some of it wasn't even that important. I told him as much and said we had time to get around to those conversations . . . a lifetime, even.

We arrived back in town after dark. He walked me to the door of my apartment, carrying my bag. When he set it down inside, he did exactly what I was expecting: he asked if he could kiss me. This time I was glad to let him.

Later that week, we had our first conversation that included the word *love*. A few days after that, he sent me a huge bouquet of red roses with a card that said, "I love you! I hope your shoes fit nicely!"

During those months, I met with a Christian counselor several times. I'd initially made contact with her to talk about my career angst, but it didn't take long for our sessions to involve conversations about Rick. As I wrestled with my never-ending expectations, she challenged me to identify and embrace God's good gifts. When the avalanche of familiar fears threatened, she reminded me of truth-telling strategies to prevent being crushed. I wrote myself a note on a four-by-six card and propped it against my computer monitor: "Accept God's good gifts. I am not trapped."

Rick always took my freak-outs in stride. Having grown up surrounded by three sisters whose age difference spans a mere five years, he wasn't rattled by female drama. He gently navigated the rough waters with me, and if I ever exasperated him, I never knew it.

Despite the roller coaster, I knew Rick was the one. Although I still sometimes wondered what God was up to, it was clear to me that he was in this relationship, that this was the way he most surely wanted me to go. I knew it was a good thing—for me and for Rick—whether I understood it all or not. After we were engaged that spring, I set another four-by-six card alongside the other: "I choose YOU! because I love you and want to build a life with you! You make me better, and I want to spend the rest of my life making yours better too!" The stream of exclamation points expressed both my embrace of God's good gifts and what I knew to be true.

I'd been wandering around the Mount Olivet Retreat Center looking for the labyrinth for nearly an hour. It was nowhere to be found. Ready to give up and go home, I turned back toward the parking lot.

At the opposite edge of the lot was a garden-like area, and just beyond that was a house. I had seen it when I arrived, and supposing it to be the caretaker's house, I hadn't explored in that direction lest I intrude on semiprivate property. But by this time, the prospect of encountering a knowledgeable person outweighed any reservations I had. *I'll give this one more try.*

I passed my car in the center of the lot as I walked toward the house. A cluster of trees separated the asphalt from an open grassy area. When I reached the other side of the trees, I saw four benches, positioned at the corners of a square space. They faced toward the center, where I barely noticed a circle bounded by bricks in the grass. The labyrinth. It was no bigger than a backyard swimming pool, its perimeter and interior path marked with bricks that lay flush with the ground. The only aboveground identification of my destination was a wooden post with a donation box and slot holding a handful of tattered guides for reflective prayer.

Leaving my backpack on one of the benches, I took a rumpled brochure and went to the edge of the circle where there was a two-foot gap between the bricks. I skimmed the guide and said aloud, "Well, here goes. I'm not expecting much, but show up, please?"

As I made my way along the winding path, I focused on the grass at my feet and reminded myself to walk slowly. Every so often, I stopped and stood for a minute just so I wouldn't finish my homework too quickly. Then I reminded myself to stop thinking about the homework: *think about the path.*

The thing about a labyrinth is that you can't get lost in it. There aren't decisions to make about which direction to go. The only decision is *to* go, to put one foot in front of the other and follow the path. Going the wrong way is never a problem. Every step forward is the right way. After my hour of taking steps in every direction but the correct one, finally walking the labyrinth was sweet relief.

At regular intervals the path switchbacked, taking me along ways I had *almost* already been—but not quite. The terrain looked the same but was a foot or two closer to the circle's center than the previous stretch had been. When I reached the first such turnaround, I thought about dead ends—the many roads to nowhere that I'd encountered in my pursuit of God's calling. As I pivoted with the labyrinth path, I had a new perspective on all those dead ends.

Maybe they were less *ends* than *beginnings*. Every "dead end" had reoriented me to go another way.

When I reached the end of the patterned path, the center of the labyrinth lay at my feet. I stopped. I stood outside the grassy circle thinking about what it meant and whether I wanted to go in. There wasn't anything to *do* there. It was a place where nothing was required of me; the path disappeared, and in its place was a circular patch of grass. If I stepped in, then what? What would I do when there was no longer any destination?

I've always been a doer. Tell me the goal and the expectations, and get out of my way. This approach to life is partly genetic, I suspect. I come from a get-it-done family. Rick is the opposite. He's a muller and comes from a family that likes to process decisions together, regardless of how long it takes.

We saw this family contrast most clearly one summer when we made a road trip to Michigan. Driving from the Twin Cities, we took the route around the north end of Lake Michigan, staying one night near Mackinaw City. My uncle had been a career historian in the Mackinaw region. As Rick and I moseyed around the area, he commented how great it would be to spend several days there with my uncle as a tour guide. That afternoon we drove to East Lansing to visit overnight with my uncle and aunt before moving on to our next destination. In the course of conversation, Rick made the same comment to them. They agreed that it sounded like a great idea.

In Rick's family, this may have been the end of it—either never coming up again or just being talked about for a long time to come. As we left East Lansing, I said to Rick, "I hope you meant what you said about vacationing with them because you just tossed that idea to a Widder." He laughed, but as I expected, within weeks, my uncle had given me his preliminary thoughts about the possibility. By summer's end, a plan for the following spring had taken shape—a plan that was successfully executed barely a year after Rick had the idea.

So as I stood outside the center of the labyrinth that July morning, I recognized that stepping into the nothing-to-do-here center was a significant decision. The only thing there was God himself. Was I willing to leave behind the *doing* for God just to *be* with him? Could I let go of my idea of what God's calling would look like and accept what it really was—what it always had been—that the destination I had really been pursuing was *God*?

A pair of birds sparred in the trees. Daylilies in a nearby bed swayed in the light breeze. My feet didn't move. I thought about the path I'd taken to this point, the life I'd lived since I was a child. Long ago I had said to God, "Whatever you want me to do, I will do it. Wherever you want me to go, I will go." I had eagerly served him, wanting him to use me and longing to hear "Well done, good and faithful servant" at the end of the road. I'd followed him every step of the way, along every bend, around every turn of the labyrinthine life I'd led—back and forth, round and round, never seeming to reach the small-*d* destination of his calling. Sometimes I had dragged my feet—kicked and screamed, even—as he had taken me places I didn't want to go.

But he would not take me to *this* place if I did not want to go, this place of *being* without *doing*. I could stand outside the center of the circle as long as I wanted to. I could even turn around and go home, cutting straight across the labyrinth path, if I so chose. No one and nothing—not even my homework—would *make* me step in.

With a deep breath, I lifted one foot over the gap between the path's end and the center of the circle. I set it down and lifted the other behind it. Once inside, I stopped again and looked around. I slowly walked the space. I stood and faced the sun. Needing to stay there for a while but not wanting to stand, I sat on one of the bricks that encircled the center rather than sit on the damp grass.

I was there to reflect on my relationship with God, but as I hugged my knees, I thought of Rick. We'd been married nearly four years by then, long enough to have seen each other's ugly sides and then find our way to new places of beauty. As I thought about the way Rick loved me, my throat tightened. He supported and encouraged everything I did, tried to do, or wanted to do—but without any expectations. If I succeeded, he loved me just the same as if I failed. What he really wanted out of our relationship was *me*. He loved simply being together.

Tears trickled down my cheeks. Some tears were for the dreams, the small-*d* destinations I'd never reached, but most were for what I hadn't quite realized so clearly until that moment—not only was *this* the destination, it was what I wanted. I wanted to know the delight of God's love for me—like a sweet peck on my cheek, like a tender look that saw through me and never wavered, like an unhurried walk together on a warm summer evening. I wanted to know the measureless Love for which Rick's love could only be a small icon.

For much of my life, I had said I wanted God to use me. Yet for all my willingness and efforts to be usable, he had not seemed to express much interest. I had wrestled with the question, If he didn't want to use me, what did he want? The more I mused over this, the more it had bothered me—that is, the actual question made me uncomfortable. *Use* me? If Rick ever said or even implied that he was "using" me, I would be crushed. If any of my friends, acquaintances, even employers talked of "using" me, I'd run the other way.

What did it say about my perception of God that I thought he wanted to "use" me? Maybe it's just semantics, but I don't think so. God doesn't want to use me as if I'm a tool to be wielded. He wants me to know him, to love him, to be with him. It seems to me that a better question to ask is, What is God doing that he's inviting me to join? In what places is he moving where I could pitch in and help? Where could I be his hands and feet, all the while enjoying his presence?

The late morning sun warmed my back as I sat on the brick boundary. It was time to go; the day's work wasn't going to do itself. I finally pushed myself up from the ground, stretched the kinks out of my back, and rolled my head to loosen my neck.

Until I had arrived at the center of the labyrinth, I thought there were two different paths—a way in and a way out. What is more, I thought the exit was a straight shot from the center to the perimeter, as if, having completed the task, I was free to leave by the most direct route possible. However, once I reached the center and looked around, I realized that the way out was the same path I had walked to get in. The center of the labyrinth was a destination and starting point all at once.

It was the destination like home is a destination—the place to which I return again and again, the place I *live* between all the places I *go*. The place that embraces me, restores me, rubs salve on my wounds, keeps me safe from all that's scary in the world. The place that enables me, every day, to live whatever the life is that God has put before me. Home is the destination that prepares me, over and over, for the journey.

Like the labyrinth path winding its way to and from the center, my journey is inextricably connected to where I find home. God has seen fit to make my physical home with Rick, till death do us part. We have an address and a mortgage together, and we hope to build a future together for a long time to come. But I am not so foolish as to think that Rick is the home I most need. His presence lightens a lot of loads, but he cannot bear the weight of my need for meaning and significance. He makes my existence better by far, but he is not and never has been the destination.

I think I've always known the destination, but we "know" things in different ways. I know that there are penguins in Antarctica, that gymnastics is a demanding sport, and that octopus probably tastes like chicken. But I've never been to the South Pole, done more than a headstand (preferably against a wall), or eaten anything with tentacles. I know it's exhilarating to win the Super Bowl and excruciating to lose a child, but I will never go through either. We have plenty of knowledge for which we have no experience.

We also "know" people in different ways. I know my neighbors, the clerk at the chocolate shop, and our tax consultant, but not at all in the way I know my family and friends. It comes down to experience together—living life in the same sphere, sharing heartbreak and joy, hope and despair.

As a junior-higher, I had written my life goal on the flyleaf of the King James Bible I'd received in second-grade Sunday school: "That I may KNOW Him." It was a goal borrowed from the apostle Paul, who told the Philippian Christians that he desired to know Christ more than anything else in life or death. I was sincere in my ambition, though I'm not exactly sure what I thought it meant to "know Christ." To some extent at least, it entailed learning about Jesus and making him happy. When I was a child, the only way I knew to do that was to obey him and serve him with my "talents."

But head knowledge, obedience, and service are just the beginning, the foundation for a lifelong journey with Jesus. It's a journey that is less about traveling from point A to point B than about daily following a path that's centered on his presence, *knowing* him. Theologians say God is omnipresent; he is everywhere. But his presence is more like a butterfly in the garden than a sky-splitting bolt of lightning. *He* is there, but often *I* am not. I do not look for his hand; I do not listen for his whisper. I am preoccupied, wandering from one goal to the next, missing the centripetal path for its subtlety.

And in that path lays God's calling. He beckons me to wind my way to and from the circle's center, over and over again. He invites me to walk the route he has laid out, doing the best I can with what he has given me, and letting him take care of the rest. What he really wants is *me*. That's all he's ever wanted.

ACKNOWLEDGMENTS

My friends are the supporting cast of this entire story. They are present on every road and side trail and in every dead end. They walk alongside me, pick me up when I stumble, and sometimes even carry me. Like George Bailey in the classic Christmas movie *It's a Wonderful Life*, I have often felt that I'm the richest (wo)man in town. Without these friends—for reasons, seasons, or a lifetime[5]—I would not be who and where I am.

And without them, this book would not be. In this regard, thanks are first due to an old-friend-turned-writing-buddy, Judy Johnson. When, in May of 2020, she wondered if I wanted to exchange essays and meet together over Zoom regularly, I could not have known the gift she was extending to me (I'm not sure she knew either). Ten new pages every other week kept my fingers on the keyboard; it's because of her that this book got finished. Besides being biweekly balm for the soul, Judy is skilled at sniffing out errant commas, misplaced modifiers, and questionable uses of "like." She is a good listener, an exceptional reader, and a dear friend.

Thanks also go to Carol Veldman Rudie, whose eye for macrostructure made her a much-appreciated conversation partner in the early stages of writing. I'm thankful too for the band of family and friends who read the completed manuscript and offered helpful perspectives: Keith and Agnes Widder, Allen Sundsmo, Cindie

Winquist, K. Kaeli Joyce, Becky Sappington, Sarah Demey, and Danielle Olander. Special thanks go to my sister Suzy, who knows the story better than most because she lived so much of it with me. She read the manuscript multiple times, and her insightful assessments helped me move forward (she is, indeed, the world's best moving buddy).

I'm also thankful for a team of new friends who walked the road of publication with me: Gisèle Mix, Kathleen Lynch, and Bree Byle. Their combined expertise made this project a reality.

My warmest thanks go to Rick, my newish best friend, who cheers my every step and has promised to walk the rest of the way with me. May God let it be so.

QUESTIONS FOR DISCUSSION OR REFLECTION

Chapter 1. The Map

1. What beliefs about God, yourself, and the world shaped your earliest years? Where and how did you learn these beliefs?
2. What are your reactions to Wendy's belief that if she served God, he would make her healthy, wealthy enough, and wise?

Chapter 2. The Trailhead

1. Reflect on your earliest years of adulthood. What expectations did you have for your future? What were your vocational goals?
2. What experiences in those years helped define you? What challenges did you face and how did you navigate them?

Chapter 3. The Fork

1. Are there ways in which your life did not go according to plan? In what ways did you have to "course correct," and what helped you decide on new directions?

2. In what ways has God pulled good surprises on you? Has he also pulled "bad" surprises on you?

Chapter 4. The Cave

1. Have you ever followed God's leading and been confused or even angry about where he took you?
2. What disappointments have you encountered professionally and in relationships? How have you navigated these low points? Are there things you would change about these hard seasons if you could?

Chapter 5. The Unmarked Trail

1. Are there ways in which your life has gone off the expected or "normal" course? What reactions to this different path have you encountered from significant people in your life?
2. How have you made decisions about the direction to go? How have you sensed God's leading?

Chapter 6. The Switchbacks

1. Have you ever struggled with panic and anxiety—and if so, can you identify the circumstances that first led to it? What are the components of your support system?
2. The black-eyed Susan was a metaphor for Wendy's dark season in Madison—"a season of darkness from which rays of light might emerge" (p. 92). What rays of light have you seen in your own seasons of darkness? Do you have a different metaphor to describe such a time?

Chapter 7. The False Peak

1. Do you have any "do life together" friendships? How were these relationships forged?
2. Describe a time you have felt betrayed—whether in a professional, religious, or personal situation. How did you respond? How was the situation resolved?

Chapter 8. The Wilderness

1. Have you ever been disappointed by a new job or a new chapter in life? Did you blame God for your circumstances? Describe your relationship to God during such a time?
2. Describe a time when you have experienced the wilderness—when you have felt cut off, alone, and as if God is being silent. What enabled you to move forward?

Chapter 9. The Avalanche

1. Has God ever put all the pieces in place for an amazing answer to prayer—and then everything has fallen apart? How did you navigate this kind of disappointment? Describe your relationship to God during such a time.
2. Wendy says God "had given me all I could take—or taken what he'd seemingly given me, depending how you look at it—and when I finally said 'I give up,' he was ready for his next move" (p. 151). Have you ever reached this place of giving up? Describe what led to it.

Chapter 10. The Dead End

1. Can you identify "belief-hypotheses" that have served as theological landmarks for your life? Are any insufficient to explain what has happened to you in your life?

2. Has God ever "seemed especially keen to remind" you that he's got everything under control, despite what your circumstances suggest (p. 161).

3. How well do you enjoy the "small-*d*" destinations? Are you able to take them as they are, or are you more inclined to expect them to be something else?

Chapter 11. The Ford

1. Have you ever been in a situation where God made the way clear by closing every door but one? What were your feelings and struggles during that time?

2. Have you experienced "shattered expectations and the ongoing difficulty of reshaping dreams" (p. 183)? Discuss your thoughts about Wendy's conclusion that moving forward at such a time is the journey of discipleship.

Chapter 12. The Labyrinth

1. Have you ever walked a labyrinth or had a different experience with Christian mysticism? What are your thoughts about and reactions to the idea of it?

2. What do you think of the popular idea that God wants to "use" us?

3. Reflect on your own journey in terms of a labyrinth with its dead ends, twists and turns—all leading to the center.

NOTES

1. Frederick Buechner, *Wishful Thinking: A Seeker's ABC*, rev. and exp. ed. (San Francisco: HarperOne, 1993), 119.

2. Walter Wangerin Jr., *Mourning into Dancing* (Grand Rapids: Zondervan, 1992).

3. Elisabeth Elliot, *A Lamp Unto My Feet: The Bible's Light for Your Daily Walk* (Ventura, CA: Regal, 2004), 229–30.

4. *You've Got Mail,* directed by Nora Ephron (Burbank, CA: Warner Bros., 1998).

5. This threefold categorization appears to derive from an essay by Brian A. "Drew" Chalker.

Wendy Widder has a PhD in Near Eastern Studies (University of the Free State), an MA in Hebrew and Semitic Studies, and an MDiv with an emphasis in educational ministries.

She is the author of two books for singles and a book for Christian school teachers, which she coauthored with her father. She has written two commentaries on the book of Daniel, *Textual Criticism of the Bible* (coauthored with Amy Anderson), and *"To Teach" in Ancient Israel: A Cognitive Linguistic Study of a Biblical Hebrew Lexical Set.*

Wendy's greatest passions are writing biblically and theologically sound materials for laypeople and teaching the Bible in an engaging way. She blogs at wendywidder.com.

Made in the USA
Columbia, SC
02 November 2022